Bitskrieg

Bitskrieg

The New Challenge of Cyberwarfare

John Arquilla

polity

First published in 2021 by Polity Press

Polity Press
65 Bridge Street
Cambridge CB2 1UR, UK

Polity Press
101 Station Landing
Suite 300
Medford, MA 02155, USA

ISBN-13: 978-1-5095-4362-5
ISBN-13: 978-1-5095-4363-2 (pb)

A catalogue record for this book is available from the British Library.

Library of Congress Cataloging-in-Publication Data
Names: Arquilla, John, author.
Title: Bitskrieg : the new challenge of cyberwarfare / John Arquilla.
Other titles: New challenge of cyberwarfare
Description: Cambridge ; Medford : Polity Press, 2021. | Includes
    bibliographical references and index. | Summary: "Pioneer of the concept
    of "netwar" explains why Bitskrieg is here to stay"-- Provided by
    publisher.
Identifiers: LCCN 2020057162 (print) | LCCN 2020057163 (ebook) | ISBN
    9781509543625 (hardback) | ISBN 9781509543632 (paperback) | ISBN
    9781509543649 (epub)
Subjects: LCSH: Cyberspace operations (Military science) | Information
    warfare. | Deterrence (Strategy) | Computer security.
Classification: LCC U167.5.C92 A77 2021 (print) | LCC U167.5.C92 (ebook)
    | DDC 355.4/1--dc23
LC record available at https://lccn.loc.gov/2020057162
LC ebook record available at https://lccn.loc.gov/2020057163

Typeset in in 11 on 13 pt Sabon
by Fakenham Prepress Solutions, Fakenham, Norfolk NR21 8NL
Printed and bound in Great Britain by TJ Books Limited

For further information on Polity, visit our website:
politybooks.com

For Peter and Dorothy Denning

The modern age has a false sense of superiority because of the great mass of data at its disposal. But the valid criterion of distinction is rather the extent to which man knows how to form and master the material at his command.

Johann Wolfgang von Goethe (1810)

Knowledge must become capability.

Carl von Clausewitz (1830)

[Cyber attacks] can actually bring us to our knees.

Admiral Mike Mullen (2011)

There are only two types of companies: Those that have been hacked and those that will be.

Robert Mueller (2012)

Contents

Acknowledgments

It has been my privilege, over the past four decades, to sit beside and learn from some of the finest minds, and individuals, dedicated to understanding the implications of the Information Age for society and security. Early on, at RAND, Willis Ware made me aware that, for all the good connectivity brings, vulnerability is its inevitable flip side. Tom Rona understood that cyberwar was going to have profound effects, one day, on battle. Captain Richard O'Neill, USN (Ret.) knew this, too, and convinced higher-ups in the Pentagon that the work my research partner David Ronfeldt and I were doing merited their support. Dick also helped found our Highlands Forum, which had a 20-year run raising awareness about Cyber-Age issues that matter. Technology journalist John Markoff and futurist Paul Saffo are both responsible for expanding my mind. As are some of the world's top hackers, especially "M" and "MHN." At the Naval Postgraduate School, Peter and Dorothy Denning, to whom this book is dedicated, have shared their insights and helped me to sharpen my thinking. As has Ryan Maness. For many years, the Honorable Leon Panetta and his wife Sylvia have welcomed me into the cyber activities of the Institute they oversee. At Polity, Louise Knight is all one could ever ask for in an editor: affirming, wise, assertive when needed.

Foreword

Communication and information lie at the heart of victory in war. The ability to communicate securely and ascertain the movements of the enemy correctly are the foundation of the safety of troops and the confidence of leadership. With the need to communicate over vaster and vaster distances, however, came hidden risks – the adversary could more easily access that information. Well-known examples are those of the Allied advantage in World War II with the successful breaking of both the German and Japanese coded battle information – the Ultra and the Magic intercepts.

Today, we have entered an even more dangerous era, an era that will call upon our entire nation's resources – material, to be sure, but moral and intellectual as well. Very small numbers of persons utilizing modern computers can deal devastating losses to advancing armies and to civilian populations. Some experts in cyberwarfare have conjectured that there may never be a final victory in cyberwars. Rather, victory may well involve merely avoiding defeat.

In the history of warfare, the initial periods when new weapons were developed were often the most dangerous. The possessors of the new technology saw themselves as having a unique advantage, but one that was fleeting, creating a "use it or lose it" mentality. It was also the period when the technology and its consequences were least understood. The result was devastation unequaled for the time.

John Arquilla's *Bitskrieg: The New Challenge of Cyberwarfare*, an eloquent and lucid study, peppered with relevant historical examples worthy of a book themselves, provides a valuable analysis that will inform both a general audience and the cyber expert. Arquilla argues that: "Cyberwar would entail changes in each of these areas: e.g., from larger formations to smaller, nimbler, highly networked units; from mass-on-mass engagements to supple swarm battle tactics; and to the larger strategic goal of 'knowing more' than the enemy – about the composition, disposition, and intentions of the forces on both sides." He brings the reader up to date on the latest advances in cyberwar – against an enemy that is anonymous, projecting force dispropor-tionate to its size, strength, or wealth.

Arquilla acknowledges that the United States projects a confirmed military superiority in its aircraft carriers and the planes that they carry, as well as a nuclear arsenal of the highest quality. But the easy access of infor-mation power on the Internet changes this advantage. A country like Iran with gunboat swarming tactics, or North Korea with cyberwarfare, can neutralize this seemingly invincible force. In the cyber domain, even small non-state actors can challenge the superpowers.

These challenges were known and feared when I served as Director of the CIA and Secretary of Defense (2009–13). Seven years, however, in the cyber era is more like a century of change in former times. So, in a manner of speaking, Arquilla picks up where my responsibilities left off. He focuses on the latest developments in cyberwarfare and the need for: secure connectivity and information; a major change in the US military and its organizational design and configuration; and a commitment to arms control negotiations related to cyber.

Regarding the security of connectivity and information, he makes a strong case for encryption and utilization of Cloud computing. In the area of military and security affairs, he argues convincingly about swarm tactics (small networked teams on the ground, connected with each other and attack aircraft) successfully engaging a larger enemy. He also emphasizes the necessity to move from a hierarchical to a networked perspective regarding information flows and organizational forms that were tailored for the industrial age, but are no longer effective today. Finally, he argues convincingly for international meetings that take seriously the idea of cyber arms control.

Indeed, Arquilla argued for cyber arms control negotiations as early as the 1990s, to no avail. At the time, the United States led the world in cyber and it was presumed that that edge would last. While the United States still has the edge offensively in the world of cyber, the Russians and the Chinese lead defensively. In fact, Arquilla argues that Iran's and North Korea's defensive capabilities in cyber are more advanced than those of the United States. And he discusses the reasons why open societies have been at a disadvantage in developing secure cyber defenses.

These are only a few of the ideas and revelations presented in this fast-paced, lively study. There is much, much more that will add depth and breadth to the reader's understanding of the cyber challenges that face the United States and the world. As Secretary of Defense, I warned that the United States was vulnerable to a cyber "Pearl Harbor." The threat of a cyber attack that shuts down our electric grid, and financial,

government, chemical, transportation, and other infrastructure systems, is real. Arquilla's handling of this
complex subject is deft and clear-eyed. His love of the
United States, and his work toward keeping us safe and
secure, place him among the leading national security
thinkers of our time. He is presenting a wake-up call to
the nation that will determine whether we are prepared
to deal with the cyber threats to the security and safety
of our democracy.

Leon E. Panetta

Preface

In the wake of the devastating Japanese attack on Pearl Harbor in December 1941, and the rain of hard blows that soon followed, American Secretary of the Navy Frank Knox mused publicly that "modern warfare is an intricate business about which no one knows everything and few know very much." Yet, within just six months, the tide turned against Japan at the Battle of Midway; and by the end of 1942 the Germans were decisively defeated in grinding land battles at El Alamein and Stalingrad. The Allies quickly learned to use aircraft carriers as the "tip of the spear" in sea fights, and that tank–plane coordination was the key to *Blitzkrieg*-style armored breakthroughs in land battles. Diffusion of the best warfighting practices happened quickly during World War II, and the methods developed in that great conflict have continued to shape much of military strategy in the more than 75 years since its end.

But swift adaptation has hardly been the case in our time, an era of emerging "postmodern" warfare. For decades, the dark, predatory pioneers of cyberwar have proved consistently able to overcome defenses and enjoy sustained freedom of action. In terms of cyberspace-based political warfare, for example, the Russians have proved masters, hitting at electoral processes in the United States and across a range of other liberal societies. Faith in the accuracy of the voting processes so vital to democracy has been undermined. China, for its part, has developed a high degree of skill at accessing and absconding with the cutting-edge intellectual property of a range of firms around the world. Mid-level powers such as North Korea have also shown considerable muscle in what might be called "strategic criminal" aspects of cyberwar, the proceeds of such larceny used to support their governments' nefarious activities, not least in the realm of nuclear weapons proliferation.

Even non-state actors of the more malevolent sort, from terrorists and militants to hacker cliques, have used cyberspace as a kind of virtual haven from which to operate. All have, one way or another, learned how to "ride the rails" of advanced technological systems, exploiting their vulnerabilities and using them as launching points for infrastructure attacks, theft of money, and more. Emergence of the Internet of Things (IoT) has only strengthened these disruptors – both hostile nations and dark networks – as now they can mobilize hundreds of millions of connected household devices to serve in their zombie networks. The current situation, far from seeing an equilibrium arise in which offensive and defensive capabilities are balanced, is one in which attackers retain the advantage because defenders rely overmuch on the least effective means of protection: Maginot-Line-like firewalls and anti-virals that are always a step behind advances in malicious software.

Clearly, one of the principal challenges today is to improve defenses. In my view, this would be by ubiquitous use of strong encryption and regular movement of data around and among the Clouds – that is, others' data systems. The Fog, consisting of the available portions and lesser-mapped areas of one's own information space and capacity, can also provide improved security, easing the fundamental problem that "data at rest are data at risk." But even a very robust remote storage and movement system cannot substitute for strong encryption; weak codes will invite acts of cyber aggression. Unfailingly.

Aside from the way poor cybersecurity leaves societies open to having both their politics and their prosperity undermined, there is another risk: that disruption of Net- and Web-connected military communications will lead to wartime disasters – in the field, at sea, and in the aerospace environment. Future battles between advanced armed forces will be incredibly fast-paced, replete with weapons empowered by artificial intelligence and coordinated to strike in networked "swarms." A military whose reflexes are slowed by the kinds of disruption computer viruses, worms and other cyber weaponry cause will find itself at risk of being outmaneuvered and swiftly defeated. This aspect of cyberwar – focused on "battle" – is the successor to World War II's *Blitzkrieg* doctrine; I call it *Bitskrieg* to draw the analogy with that crucially important previous inflection point in military and security affairs.

The dangers posed by the more familiar aspects of cyberwar, from political disruption to criminal hacking and potential infrastructure attacks, pale next to the consequences of failing to see that military operations can be fatally undermined by information insecurity. That is why the need to start paying serious, effective attention to armed-conflict aspects of cyberwar is urgent. But the scope and variety of cyber threats are daunting, making it difficult to address all, especially given the attention-grabbing nature of the latest incident of one sort or another. This suggests that there is one more important, also unmet, challenge that should be taken up alongside efforts to improve cybersecurity and prepare to wage *Bitskrieg*-style field operations: arms control. Since virtually all advanced information technology is "multi-use" – employable for commerce, provision of services, social interaction *or* war – the nuclear model of counting missiles and controlling fissile material will no longer do. This has led many (well, most) to scoff at the very idea of cyber arms control. But there is another paradigm that is based on behavior, rather than "bean counting." It has worked well, for many decades, with the Chemical and Biological Weapons Conventions – covering types of deadly arms whose basic materials can be fabricated by countless countries – whose signatories have covenanted never to make or use such devices. A similar, behavior-based approach to cyber arms control is possible as well.

The need to protect individuals, intellectual property, infrastructures and elections from cyber attack is hardly new; the way to meet challenges to them that I advance is. "New" in the sense that the current approach to cybersecurity, so reliant on firewalls and anti-virals, should for the most part be jettisoned in favor of the strongest encryption and the widespread use of Cloud and Fog computing. The failure of existing security systems is so overwhelming, as the reader will see, that the need to shift to a new security paradigm is now well beyond urgent. As a wise American chief of naval operations once said to me about cyber threats, "The red light is flashing."

And, with armed forces and armed conflict in mind, I argue herein that the direct, warfighting implications of advanced information technologies – including artificial intelligence – have received too little attention for far too long. The fundamental problem is that a wide range of these new tools have simply been folded into or grafted onto older practices. Thus, the shift from *Blitzkrieg* to *Bitskrieg* has not yet been made. My goal is to make sure that aggressors don't make this leap first. The painful lessons inflicted by the Nazi war machine from 1939 to 1941, at the outset of the Mechanization Age, should sensitize us to the potential cost of failing to parse the profound implications for warfare posed by the Computer Age. A cost that will surely be imposed should cyber challenges to society and security remain unmet.

Aside from illuminating the current challenges that must be met and mastered if peace and prosperity are to have a reasonable chance of thriving as we look ahead, I also "look back" in two principal ways. One aspect of this retrospection focuses on linking current – and future – issues in military affairs and information security systems to what has gone before. The best example of this tie to earlier history is the manner in which, during World War II, the Allies, using the world's first high-performance computers, "hacked" the Axis and won critical victories in desperate times, often when the odds were stacked heavily in favor of the aggressors, as at the Battle of Midway in June 1942. The knowledge advantage that the Allies possessed over the Axis played a crucial role in the latter's defeat. Clearly, mastery of the information domain has long mattered; it matters just as much to victory today, and will only grow in importance over the coming decades.

The second way in which I engage in retrospection reflects my own experiences and ideas in this field over the past 30-plus years, in war and peace. As I look back, from early debates about the strategic implications of the Information Age *circa* 1990 to very recent times, I find that, Forrest-Gump-like, I have been present at many high-level American policy debates about the various dimensions of cyberwar, and have sometimes played an active role in events.

The reflective passages, the reader will find, offer a range of first-time revelations about: how the information advantage over Saddam Hussein enabled General Norman Schwarzkopf to opt for the daring "left hook" plan that was the heart of Operation Desert Storm; why the 78-day air campaign during the Kosovo War did so little damage to Serbian forces; what went on at the first Russo-American meeting of cyber experts; and where the current debates about the military uses of artificial intelligence are, and where they are headed. It has been a privilege to be involved in these and a range of other cyber-related events over the years. But having a privilege is hardly the same as witnessing real progress, and of the latter I have seen far too little. Perhaps this book will stimulate a renewed, and broader, discourse about cyberwar before the Age of *Bitskrieg* opens with a thunderclap upon us. I hope so.

John Arquilla
Monterey, December 2020

1

"Cool War" Rising

The German philosopher of war, Carl von Clausewitz, described armed conflict as "a true chameleon" whose three base elements are "primordial violence . . . the play of chance," and, ultimately, its "subordination as an instrument of policy."[1] He had no way of knowing, some two centuries ago, how prescient his notion of the chameleon-like character of warfare would prove to be in its Information-Age incarnation. Echoing Clausewitz, strategist Martin Libicki has described cyber conflict as a "mosaic of forms" ranging across the various modes of military operations, and having significant psychological, social, political, and economic aspects as well. As to Clausewitz's element of primordial violence, Libicki has contended that cyberwarfare slips the bonds of traditional thinking about armed conflict. Of its many manifestations, he has argued, "None of this requires mass, just guile."[2] This poses some very major challenges to those who would defend against cyber attacks, given that the lack of requirement for mass means that small nations, networks of hackers, even super-empowered smart individuals unmoored from any Clausewitzian notion of a guiding policy, can wage a variety of forms of warfare – operating from virtually anywhere, striking at virtually any targets.

Cyber attackers, whoever and wherever they are, can opt to disrupt the information systems upon which armed forces' operations increasingly depend – on land, at sea, in the air, even in orbit – or take aim at the control systems that run power, water, and other infrastructures in countries around the world. This mode of attack can also foster crime, enabling the theft of valuable data – including cutting-edge intellectual property – from commercial enterprises, the locking-up of information systems whose restoration can then be held for ransom, or simply the exploitation or sale of stolen identities. The democratic discourse can easily be targeted as well, allowing a whole new incarnation of political warfare to emerge in place of classical propaganda – as demonstrated in the 2016 presidential election in the United States,[3] but which can be employed to disrupt free societies anywhere in the world. And for those attackers of a more purely nihilistic bent, controlled or stolen identities can be conscripted into huge "zombie" armies deployed to mount distributed denial-of-service (DDoS) attacks aimed at overwhelming the basic ability to operate of the targeted systems – institutional, commercial, or individual. When billions of household appliances, smartphones, and embedded systems (including implanted locator chips in pets) that constitute the Internet of Things (IoT) are added as potential "recruits" for cyber attackers' robot networks ("botnets"), the offensive potential of cyberwarfare seems close to limitless.

And all this takes, as Libicki has sagely observed, is *guile*. Thus, it seems that, aside from providing a strong affirmation of Clausewitz's general point about conflict having chameleon-like properties, the many faces of cyberwar undermine his three base elements. There is no need to commit acts of overarching violence, or even for a connection to higher-level policy, when, for example, millions of "smart refrigerators," designed to send their owners an email when they need milk, can be hacked, controlled, and ordered to overwhelm their targets with millions of emails. As to chance, the vast range of targets available to cyber attackers – who often remain hidden behind a veil of anonymity, a "virtual sanctuary" – suggests that luck is a much less included factor. This undermining of Clausewitz's base elements leads to a serious challenge to his firmly held belief that "defense is a stronger form of fighting than attack."[4] This was certainly the case in his time, when defense-in-depth defeated Napoleon in Russia, and later saw the Duke of Wellington's "thin red line" decimate the *Grande Armée* at Waterloo. A century later, the costly failed offensives on the Western Front in World War I affirmed the wisdom of Clausewitz. And even the brief period of *Blitzkrieg*'s success in World War II gave way, from El Alamein to Stalingrad to the Battle of the Bulge, before stout defenses. But, two centuries since Clausewitz, the rise of cyberwar is now upending his unwavering belief in defense dominance. Instead, offense rules.

To date, the best-known manifestations of cyberwar have emerged in the personal and commercial realms. Hundreds of millions of people around the world have had their privacy compromised, either by direct hacks or by having their information stolen from insurance, financial, retail, social media, and government databases. With regard to ostensibly "secure" government databases, even these have proved porous. The most notorious incident was acknowledged by the US Office of Personnel Management in June 2015. Of this intrusion, in which hackers accessed sensitive personal information, the President of the American Federation of Government Employees, James Cox, asserted "all 2.1 million current federal employees and an additional 2 million federal retirees and former employees" were affected.[5] (My own classified personnel file was among those hacked.) As the matter was investigated further, the estimated number of persons affected quintupled, to more than 20 million, according to Congressional testimony of the then-Director of the Federal Bureau of Investigation, James Comey, given just a month later.[6] But even this staggering breach paled in comparison with the revelation in May 2019 that *nearly 900 million* sensitive financial records had been hacked from the database of the First American Title Company.[7]

As to the theft of intellectual property and other types of exploitative or disruptive cyber attacks aimed at commercial enterprises, these cause more than 1 trillion dollars ($US) in damages each year. University research centers are also targeted as, according to one tactful report, they "haven't historically been as attentive to security as they should be."[8] While the ransoming of locked-up information currently accounts for less than 1% of annual losses, this mode of attack is growing at a steep rate.[9] Often, such theft and extortion aim at serving causes beyond just enrichment of the malefactors. In the case of North Korea's cyber crimes, the United Nations has reported that the roughly $2 billion gained as of mid-2019, by attacks on banks and crypto-currency (e.g., Bitcoin, Ethereum, Ripple) exchanges, has been used to support its nuclear weapons program.[10] This illicit form of fundraising lies somewhere between theft and statecraft. Call it "strategic crime." Much as, in the sixteenth century, Queen Elizabeth I tacitly encouraged her piratical "sea dogs" to prey upon maritime commerce to help fill Britain's coffers. Strategic crime has long played a role in statecraft via this form of naval irregular warfare.[11]

Clearly, when it comes to the abovementioned modes of cyber attack, offense is currently quite dominant. And, as George Quester's seminal study of stability and instability of the international system notes, when the apparent risks and costs of taking the offensive are low, conflicts of all sorts are more likely to proliferate.[12] They may be small-scale, individually, but their cumulative effects are large – and growing – as opposed to the more purely military realm, in which the patterns of development and diffusion are less apparent. So much so that, to some analysts, the emergence of militarized cyberwar seems highly unlikely.[13]

Cyber attacks in armed conflicts *have* had a lower profile, but there are some troubling examples – most provided by Russia. In 2008, when Russian troops and Ossetian irregulars invaded Georgia, the defenders' information systems and links to higher commands were compromised by cyber attacks on their communications. Panic-inducing mass messaging aimed at people's phones and computers in areas where the Russians were advancing put large, disruptive refugee flows onto the roads, clogging them when Georgian military units were trying to move into blocking positions. All this helped Russia to win a lop-sided victory *in five days*.[14]

More recently, two other aspects of cyberwar have come to the fore in the conflict in Ukraine between government forces and separatists in Donetsk, with the latter supported not only by Russian irregulars – "little green men," so named for the lack of identifying patches on their uniforms – but also by bits and bytes at the tactical and strategic levels. In the field, Ukrainian artillery units were for some time victimized by hacks into their soldiers' cellphone apps that were being used to speed up the process of calling in supporting fire.

Russian-friendly hackers helped to geo-locate artillery batteries by this means, and brought down counter-battery fire upon them. The result: diminution of Ukrainian artillery effectiveness, although the precise extent of losses incurred remains a matter of some debate.[15]

At a more strategic level, the Russo-Ukrainian conflict has also featured a number of troubling attacks. The first came on Ukraine's electrical power grid infrastructure in December 2015, when 30 substations in the Ivano-Frankivsk *oblast* were shut down as hackers took over their highly automated system control and data acquisition (SCADA) equipment. Nearly a quarter of a million Ukrainians were affected by this hack, which has been attributed to "Sandworm," a Russian army cyber-warrior unit. These same hackers are believed to have masterminded the extensive cyber attacks on Ukrainian finance, government, and (once again) power companies in June 2017.

Ostensibly, this latter operation aimed at freezing data, whose unlocking was then held for ransom. But the attacks, which did some collateral damage in other countries, were more likely intended simply to impose costly disruptions – and perhaps to serve as launching pads for covert insertions of malicious software designed to act as virtual "sleeper cells," waiting for their activation at some later date. Overall, the costs inflicted by these 2017 attacks exceeded $10 billion, according to the estimate of Tom Bossert, then a senior Trump Administration cybersecurity official.[16] These uses of cyberwar as a means of "strategic attack" are highly concerning, especially the demonstration that SCADA systems – in wide and increasing use throughout the world – are vulnerable to being taken over.

Russian cyber operations in Georgia and Ukraine should be seen as among the first "capability tests" that have provided glimpses of what future cyberwars may look like. Just as the Spanish Civil War (1936–9) foreshadowed the kinds of actions – from tank maneuvers in the field to the aerial bombardment of cities – that were to characterize much of the fighting in World War II under the rubric of *Blitzkrieg*,[17] so too have recent Russian uses of the various modes of cyberwar in Georgia and Ukraine provided a glimpse of the next "face of battle": *Bitskrieg.*

And, just as fascist forces in Spain – including tens of thousands of German and Italian volunteers – demonstrated the synergy of armored and aerial operations brought into close coordination by radio, today Russian "volunteers" in Donetsk are proving that integrated cyber and physical operations have profound effects. Another goal of the *Blitzkrieg* doctrine as practiced by the Germans early in World War II was "to disrupt [the enemy's] lines of communication."[18] The importance of gaining an information edge by disabling the opponent's command systems was a central thesis of Heinz Guderian, a pioneer of *Blitzkrieg*. No surprise that he began his career as a signals officer, nor that he played a major role in the swift victory over France in 1940, which, as Karl-Heinz Frieser has observed, "caused outdated doctrines to collapse; the nature of war was revolutionized."[19] *Bitskrieg*, too, will likely one day cause the collapse of outdated doctrines.

Bitskrieg is also similar to its World War II-era predecessor in terms of its emphasis on, and capability for, waging political warfare. For another element of *Blitzkrieg* doctrine was the employment of propaganda and subversion to prepare for invasion by field forces. This practice, too, had origins in Spain's Civil War, as fascist General Emilio Mola, whose troops were closing in on Madrid from four directions, said that his advance was aided by a covert, subversive "fifth column."

The early German annexations of Austria and Czechoslovakia benefited tremendously from such fifth-columnist actions, as was also the case in the 1940 invasion of Norway – a daring operation whose success, in part, was due to the activities of Vidkun Quisling and other Nazi collaborators. Their effects were so substantial that, as William L. Shirer noted, the capital Oslo "fell to little more than a phantom German force dropped from the air at the local, undefended airport." And at strategically important Narvik, the initial defending force "surrendered to the Germans without firing a shot."[20] An Anglo-French force landed at Narvik later – too late, despite much hard fighting, to overturn the final result of this campaign.

In our time, we have the example of a "virtual fifth column" employed to great effect by the Russians, disrupting the Ukrainian ability to resist aggression in, and annexation of, the Crimea. At the same time, a parallel fifth column was used to spread propaganda justifying this invasion to the wider world. This approach, which included a "people's plebiscite" – a tactic employed by the Nazis – helped to ensure that the Russian take-over would be bloodless, allowed to consolidate with neither effective internal resistance by the Ukrainian government nor international military counter-intervention. In this instance, the Russian *fait accompli* froze the principal Western guarantors of Ukrainian territorial integrity – per the terms of the 1994 Budapest Memorandum on Security Assurances: Britain, the United States, and France – into almost complete inaction.

But cyber-based political warfare can do far more than just provide support for invasions; it can also be used, as the Russians have done, to foment unrest and chaos in the United States and other open societies that are inherently vulnerable to the dissemination of lies cloaked as truth. Yet political warfare is not only suited to undermining democracies; it can also attack authoritarian and totalitarian rulers. In the 1980s, for example, prior to when the Internet began its rapid growth, President Ronald Reagan pursued an information strategy via radio and direct-broadcast satellite that put pressure on the Soviet Union and its control of Eastern Europe. Indeed, the argument has been advanced that his initiative played a significant role in the peaceful end of the Cold War and dissolution of the Soviet Union.[21] Today, cyberspace-based connectivity provides even greater opportunities for striking at dictators. Social media links *billions* of people, a significant slice of whom live under controlling regimes. Authoritarians are aware of this, and mount efforts to monitor – sometimes to close down – access to such media. They may succeed – for a while. But advancing technology continues a major trend toward broader, easier connectivity, making it ever harder to control access. If past is prologue, even the harshest control efforts will ultimately fail. During the Second World War, John Steinbeck's *The Moon is Down*, a novel of resistance, made its way in bootleg translations to virtually every occupied country, inspiring opposition to Nazi rule.[22] Information diffusion today is much easier; its effects are likely to be at least as powerful and widespread. Probably much more so, for the classic theme of active resistance resonates in and from the virtual realm in ways that mobilize "the real world" – evinced in recent decades by the "color revolutions" and the Arab Spring.

Back in World War II, physical resistance featured widely varied acts of sabotage against the Nazis' transport, communications, and arms manufacturing infrastructures – despite often quite terrible reprisals being inflicted upon innocent civilians. Perhaps the most important of the sabotage campaigns was that mounted by Norwegian resistance fighters who prevented shipping of heavy-water supplies – essential to the Nazi nuclear program – from Norway to Germany. One of the key leaders of the Nazi effort to build an atomic bomb, the physicist Kurt Diebner, confirmed that "It was the elimination of German heavy-water production in Norway that was the main factor in our failure to achieve a self-sustaining atomic reactor before the war ended."[23] Inspiring messages, conjuring visions like the one crafted in Steinbeck's *The Moon Is Down*, provided informational support that helped to catalyze and sustain such heroic acts of resistance. This was despite the strict controls the Nazis imposed on communications.

Today, it is very difficult to prevent information flows, in a sustained and leakproof way, from reaching mass publics. And the same technologies that allow for "information blockades" to be evaded offer up many opportunities for engaging in active resistance as well. Thus, sabotage using explosives – still quite an available option – can now be augmented by acts of virtual disruption in the form of what I call "cybotage." Beyond the usual denial-of-service attacks, the worms, and varieties of malicious software designed to disrupt information flows and functions, or to corrupt databases, it is also increasingly possible to employ bits and bytes that cause physical damage to important equipment. The watershed example of this kind of cybotage was the Stuxnet worm that attacked the system running Iranian centrifuges, forcing them to spin themselves at such a high rate that it led to their self-destruction. As General Michael Hayden, the former head of the National Security Agency and the Central Intelligence Agency, put the matter, "Previous cyberattacks had effects limited to other computers . . . This is the first attack of a major nature in which a cyberattack was used to effect physical destruction."[24] In a way, the Stuxnet operation – widely assumed to have been conceived by the United States and Israel – was like the Norwegian commando attacks on German heavy-water facilities and supplies during World War II: both actions were aimed at slowing the progress of nascent nuclear programs.

Stuxnet destroyed those centrifuges in 2010 – though it was most likely implanted into the Iranian system years earlier, lying in wait, activated at a moment when it brought the blessing of time for negotiations in a burgeoning proliferation crisis. A preliminary arms control agreement was reached in 2013, and formalized as the "Joint Comprehensive Plan of Action" in 2015. It was adhered to until the United States withdrew from the agreement in 2018. The Iranians openly broke the terms of the agreement in 2019. But long before this break, in 2012, Tehran and/or Iranian-aligned hackers demonstrated a capacity for retaliatory cybotage, too. Shamoon, a virus that attacked the master boot records – key to mass storage and computer function – erased and irremediably overwrote key data on more than 30,000 PCs of the oil firm Saudi Aramco. A similar attack was launched soon after against the Qataris, further contributing to widespread concern about the vulnerability of a key aspect of the global oil industry to cybotage.[25] Needless to say, the Iranians have denied any involvement in Shamoon – much as the United States and Israel have never acknowledged any role in Stuxnet. The covert and clandestine aspect of cyberwar relies on veils of anonymity and deniability, for real, "smoking gun" evidence of actual involvement or perpetration would likely lead to escalation – perhaps even to a shooting war.

As to Stuxnet itself, even though it was carefully inserted into an Iranian system and designed for a very specific target – the programmable logic controls on particular Siemens equipment – its properties gave it a broader functionality across a range of SCADA systems. And when the worm leaked "into the wild," perhaps spread by a technician who picked it up inadvertently (or not) on a flash drive, Stuxnet variants began to turn up. In 2011, Duqu emerged. Intended for intrusion and intelligence-gathering, it had Stuxnet-style attack properties as well. The following year, yet another variant debuted, Flame, which apparently attacked the Iranian oil industry. More recently, Triton appeared in 2017, and very quickly demonstrated a Stuxnet-like ability to disable safety systems, this time at a Saudi petrochemical plant. In the worst case, this attack could have caused an explosion leading to mass casualties and a major environmental hazard. Thankfully, it was detected before this happened; subsequent forensic investigation pointed to Triton having come from Russia. A wider search to detect this Stuxnet variant revealed that it is still spreading around the world.[26] Other acts of cybotage using different malware have been alleged as well – as in Venezuelan government charges that the United States attacked its infrastructure as part of a "regime change" effort. While lacking credibility, such charges frame a growing fear of an emerging "cool war."

What makes these exploits "cool"? There are two things, I believe. First, the actions taken must be clandestine (completely hidden), covert (if detected, deniable as to the real perpetrator), or at least able to be denied for a time and in a manner that forestalls retaliatory action. Second, cool war operations should be largely limited to disruption – even costly disruption – inflicting little, oftentimes no, destruction or loss of life. These two factors characterize actions taken in the fictional conflict Frederik Pohl depicted in his 1981 novel *The Cool War*. He was quite prescient, a decade before the Internet took off, including such actions by covert operators as causing stock market crashes and big drops in commodity values.[27] Non-military forms of cyberwar considered thus far fit the category of "cool." From strategic crime to spying, and on to cybotage, perpetrators are often able to protect their anonymity for long periods – some without ever being reliably identified or counterattacked. As Joseph Nye has observed, "retaliatory threats of punishment are less likely to be effective in cyberspace, where the identity of the attacker is uncertain; there are many unknown adversaries."[28] And the fact that, to be "cool," attacks have to disrupt much but destroy little, means the likelihood of escalation to wider war is minimized. Even so, as Pohl foresaw in his novel, a *lot* of small-scale disruption can lead to a virtually unlivable world.

More war, less violence?

There is yet another aspect of "cool" that applies to cyberwar: the portion of that word's meaning that can be used to describe something subtly attractive, insightful, or innovative. This is the kind of cool that speaks to cyberwar as David Ronfeldt and I first envisioned it at RAND back in the early 1990s. For us, "cyber" meant more than just cyberspace. We drew from the Greek root *kybernan*, "to steer," and aligned ourselves with Norbert Wiener's notion of cybernetics as the process of control through feedback.[29] Our view was that, in military affairs, technological advances in information systems – communications, sensing, weapons guidance, and automation – implied the possibility of catalyzing transformational changes in warfare, particularly in battle doctrine. We saw in having an "information edge" the chance to defeat larger forces with smaller, nimbler, more networked units – on land, at sea, and in the air. Oddly enough, our views were shaped quite a bit by the example of the thirteenth-century Mongol campaigns of conquest. Genghis Khan's "hordes" – often smaller than the armies they faced – benefited immeasurably from what we today call near-real-time reporting on the disposition, composition, and movements of the enemy by their corps of "Arrow Riders," a Pony-Express-like communication system that gave the Khan a consistent winning advantage.

To be sure, Ronfeldt and I also perceived, back then, the tremendous broad potential of "information-related conflict at a grand level," which would include new manifestations of "propaganda and psychological campaigns, political and cultural subversion . . . interference with local media [and covert] infiltration of computer networks and databases." Clearly, in the more than quarter-century since we wrote those words, our predictions about the rise of political warfare and cyberspace-based disruption have been borne out. But we had an even deeper concern, driven by the fast-growing dependence of advanced militaries on information systems of all sorts. Our belief was that these technological advances were going to usher in an era of armed conflict in which the side with better information – that could be refined into *knowledge* to guide tactical and strategic decision making – was going to be able to win remarkable, lop-sided victories with fewer, but far better guided, forces. We saw it as a world in which, for the side with the edge in the information domain, "[s]mall numbers of light, highly mobile forces defeat and compel the surrender of large masses of heavily armed, dug-in enemy forces, *with little loss of life on either side.*"[30] This possibility of less bloody, yet more decisive, operations lies at the heart of the more purely military aspect of cyberwar: *Bitskrieg.*

The new mode of warfare, in this respect, echoes the decisiveness of early *Blitzkrieg* campaigns in World War II that were energized by tank-and-plane operations, closely coordinated by radio – the key information technology of the time. For example, the German invaders of France in the spring of 1940 won, in just several weeks, an amazing victory at relatively low cost in killed and wounded – on both sides. As John Keegan described the rapid German breakthrough and swift conclusion of the campaign, it "had been, in its last weeks, almost a war of flowers."[31] In Yugoslavia, during the spring of the following year, the Germans defeated the million-man defending army in 10 days, suffering only 151 battle deaths. The advance on Belgrade had been led by the 41st Panzer Corps, which lost *only 1 soldier* killed in action.[32] Similar successes accompanied operations in Russia and North Africa, until the Germans became bogged down in set-piece battles at Stalingrad and El Alamein – both of which they lost. Thereafter, Allied field commanders such as Russia's Marshal Zhukov and the American General Patton showed how they, too, could operate in swift, decisive *Blitzkrieg*-like fashion. In later iterations of this mode of conflict, the Israelis won a lightning war against an Arab coalition in 6 days in 1967, then the Indians achieved a decisive victory over Pakistan in 1971 in 13 days – Field-Marshal Lord Carver called the latter campaign "a true *Blitzkrieg.*" The same can be said of the Six-Day War.[33]

Yet, when Desert Storm came along in 1991, something very different emerged in the campaign to liberate Kuwait from the large, modern Iraqi Army – so recently battle-tested in eight, ultimately successful, years of bloody fighting against Iran. The Iraqis were also abundantly equipped with Russian artillery that outranged American guns, and well trained in both Soviet and Western theories of modern maneuver warfare. In fact, the very area in which General Schwarzkopf's famous armored "left hook" was launched had served as Iraq's principal training ground for tank commanders. Despite all this, the Allied ground offensive defeated an Iraqi field army of over 50 divisions in just four days, the victors suffering the loss of only 148 killed in action. Over 70,000 Iraqi soldiers were taken prisoner. The reason for this result: the Iraqis had to "fight blind," while Allied forces knew where virtually all enemy units were positioned, where there were gaps in their artillery coverage, and where and when they tried to move. It was an information edge that made an enormous difference. Despite this, in the planning of Desert Storm, it was not fully appreciated early on. At the time (August 1990 – February 1991), I was a member of the small RAND strategic analysis team working for General Schwarzkopf, and had become completely convinced that the huge Allied advantage in intelligence, surveillance, and reconnaissance (ISR) meant that the boldest maneuvers could be executed – in this instance, a flanking movement around the *entire* Iraqi position in Kuwait – with little risk and even less bloodshed.

But many senior officers advocated for a more direct approach, and strongly opposed the case for the wide "left hook," which they thought too risky. A heated debate ensued that went on for weeks. Ultimately, General Schwarzkopf chose to believe in the power of the Allied information edge and sided with those who favored a major flanking movement; the results bore out his judgment. And the Allied edge was not only in sensing and communications; it also extended to the increased "information content" of weapons as well, whose guidance systems made them far more lethal than in any previous conflict. Colonel Kenneth Allard summed up the reasons for this "turning point" victory in military affairs:

> Computer-assisted weapons intended to kill at great ranges with a single shot were now the stock-in-trade of the frontline soldier. He was supported by commanders and staffs who used "battle management" systems to monitor the status of enemy forces, friendly forces, and the all-important movement of logistics. Strategic direction in the form of information, intelligence, orders, and advice arrived in a river of digital data that flowed incessantly.[34]

In the wake of my work on Desert Storm, I brought insights from this experience to my colleague David Ronfeldt, appearing at his office door one afternoon to say, "I have one word for you, David: 'Cyberwar.'" And so we were off to the races, striving to make the case for truly revolutionary change in military affairs.

We found a few defense intellectuals who accepted our logic about the concrete value of having an information edge. A useful analogy was the thought experiment I suggested about a chess game between two players of equal strength, but with one side limited in vision to seeing only his or her own pieces. An opposing piece would reveal itself only in making a capture or when a friendly piece stumbled upon it. In such a situation, could the side with the information edge win with fewer pieces? If so, how many fewer? Invariably, the answers were that the fully sighted side could do without much of the traditional full complement of pieces. Thus, the issue of assessing the material value of an information edge began to come into focus as a matter of serious enquiry.

The most influential defense official who appreciated this point was the Director of Net Assessment, the legendary Pentagon strategist Andrew Marshall. He and others in his orbit soon began to champion the notion of a "revolution in military affairs" (RMA) – in part based on the informational dimension, in part on other emerging technologies and their implications for organizational redesign and doctrinal innovation. But most individuals in the military establishment recoiled from the word "revolution," making pursuit of a true RMA difficult. Cyberwar languished. Then, as evolution of the Net and the Web quickened, the cyberwar concept itself was narrowed just to operations in and from the virtual domain – neglecting its physical warfighting dimension. The narrowing had great appeal.

The most important early advocates of this way of thinking about cyberwar came from the communities of experts in nuclear strategy and air power; naturally, their habits of mind led them to conceive of cyberspace-based operations as a form of strategic attack on a nation's cities and critical infrastructures. Much as they had played a significant role in parsing the complexities of nuclear strategy and air power for generations, RAND experts now came to the fore in developing these much more limited views of cyber strategy as well – most notably in the team led by Roger Molander, whose study *Strategic Information Warfare* and the table-top wargame exercises developed therefrom proved highly influential.[35]

Needless to say, this approach ignored the notion of *Bitskrieg* as a possible next face of battle. What followed were several years of technical speculations about how to take down power grids, seize control of SCADA systems, and create widespread psychological effects akin to those sought by Klaatu, the cool alien emissary, when he shut down virtually all the world's power systems for half an hour in the original film version (1951) of *The Day the Earth Stood Still*.[36]

Klaatu aside – in the original film, it's not clear that his demonstration of disruptive power would work to gain humanity's compliance with his demand that Earthmen not bring their violent ways into space – Ronfeldt and I have always bristled at the evolving emphasis on cyberwar as simply a strategic "weapon of mass disruption." This manifestation of cyberwar has none of the horror that attends nuclear conflict – a threatened holocaust that has led to deterrence stability under the rubric of "mutual assured destruction" (MAD). And to the extent to which this "strategic" view of cyberwar is associated with the notion of victory through conventional aerial bombing, it only needs to be noted that very few air campaigns – if any – have ever achieved their aims politically, militarily, or psychologically.[37] Instead, as Ronfeldt and I have argued for decades, the notion that cyberwar is key to a new "strategic attack paradigm" – the term introduced by James Adams[38] – will ultimately prove to be a grave error, engendering ruinous costs for little results. We strove to make an alternate case, favoring far more tactical-level uses of information systems to empower forces in the field, at sea, and in the aerospace environment, to enable them to make the shift to *Bitskrieg*.

The first significant opportunity to wage this sort of cyberwar came in Kosovo in 1999, when NATO sought to end a predatory campaign conducted by the Serbs against the Kosovars. I served on a team advising the then-Chairman of the Joint Chiefs of Staff, General Henry "Hugh" Shelton. We proposed a plan of campaign that focused on inserting key elements of our Special Forces into the Kosovo Liberation Army (KLA). The idea being that elite US Army Green Berets, working closely on the ground with the Kosovars, and linked to the ISR network – as well as to air and missile strike forces – could find and target Serb forces swiftly, reliably, *lethally*. Shelton embraced the idea of having the Special Forces fight alongside the KLA. However, the opportunity was forgone, for the most part, because of sharp criticism of and concern about the risks entailed in this approach. Instead, NATO leaders argued that the air-only operation was "making real progress," that guerrilla-style operations would not work, and stuck to their stated preference for a far larger force to be deployed if there were to be *any* boots on the ground.[39] President Clinton sided with the NATO position. The air-only campaign proceeded for 78 days, during which Serb field forces suffered very little damage, and the bombing caused serious civilian casualties – sparking widespread international criticism. But Belgrade did finally agree to withdraw from Kosovo.

Kosovo was a case, as Ivo Daalder and Michael O'Hanlon labeled it, of "winning ugly."[40] It was also a missed opportunity to wage the first full-blown *Bitskrieg* using our vision. To some degree, the KLA formations did force the Serbs to move about, and enabled attack aircraft to detect, track, and strike at them. But not nearly often enough – a broader presence of Green Berets with them was needed to give the insurgents the kind of strong connectivity with NATO that would have allowed for swifter and far more accurate close air support. Ronfeldt and I were disappointed; but soon after the Kosovo War's end we were allowed to share our thoughts publicly about the path that we believed should be followed in future military campaigns.[41] And we didn't have to wait too long to see a much more fully realized version of our concept put into practice. In the wake of the 9/11 attacks on America, it was quickly determined that al Qaeda had perpetrated them, and that the Taliban government of Afghanistan was providing that terrorist group with a physical haven. There was no time to muster a large ground force; and arranging to send big units to that land-locked country swiftly, then supplying them, would have been nightmarish. So, instead, only 11 "A-teams" of Green Berets went to Afghanistan in late 2001 – just under 200 soldiers.

They soon linked up with friendly Afghans of the Northern Alliance, a group that had been previously beaten quite soundly by the Taliban, losing roughly 95 percent of the country to those fundamentalist zealots. But with the leavening of those few Americans, who were highly networked with air assets, they managed to defeat al Qaeda and drive the Taliban from power in very short order.[42] *This*, Ronfeldt and I believed, was a true demonstration of the power of being able to employ a major information advantage that would allow far smaller forces to defeat much greater enemy armies. And to win even when indigenous allies' forces are of a far lesser quality, man for man, than the enemy they face. Thus, the defeated, demoralized fighters of the Northern Alliance reemerged victorious – because the handful of American specialists who fought alongside them on horseback were uplinked to ISR and attack aircraft that allowed them to monitor enemy movements in real time and to call in strikes from the air, in minutes, from the steady and unending stream of fighter-bomber pilots who maintained constant coverage above the battlespace. Then-Secretary of Defense Donald Rumsfeld, who had unleashed the Green Berets over the objections of many senior generals, saw in this campaign the singular opportunity to catalyze what he came to call "military transformation."[43]

It turned out that Pentagon leaders disliked the word "transformation" as much as they hated the notion of a "revolution" in military affairs. And in the debate over the looming invasion of Iraq in 2003, they prevailed against Donald Rumsfeld's preferred idea of using the "Afghan model" – a few highly networked troops inserted into indigenous rebel groups (Kurds in the north and Shiites in the south, in this case) – in favor of a more traditional armored attack, augmented by "shock and awe" strategic bombing of Iraqi infrastructure. The campaign unfolded in *Blitzkrieg*-like fashion, hewing to a playbook Heinz Guderian's World War II-era panzer leaders would easily recognize. John Keegan made this point in his study of the campaign, noting that the invasion "was predicated on the principle of [coalition forces] advancing at the highest possible speed, brushing aside resistance and halting to fight only when absolutely necessary."[44] In the event, conventional military operations went well, but a nasty insurgency soon arose that bedeviled the occupiers for years. And, as *more* troops were sent, they provided more targets for improvised explosives and snipers. Large reinforcements were sent as well to Afghanistan – overturning Rumsfeld's model – which had remained relatively quiet for four years, but then insurgents arose there, too. The *Blitzkrieg* playbook proved useless in both countries, where US and Allied forces soon suffered from *enlisement*, the term the French used when they were bogged down in Indochina.

This brings us to the matter of how cyberwar applies to countering insurgency and terrorism. As important as an information edge is in conventional warfare, it is crucial in irregular conflicts. For without information, refined into actionable knowledge, it is simply too hard to *find*, much less to fight, elusive foes. Cyberwar, which emphasizes the informational dimension, offers two remedies: hack the enemy, and turn one's own forces into a "sensory organization." They can still be "shooters," too, but "sensors" first. As Paul Van Riper and F. G. Hoffman put the issue – about what will matter most in 21st-century conflict – "what really counts in war is gaining and maintaining a relative advantage in . . . awareness."[45]

Lack of knowledge about enemy dispositions, movements, and intentions was the cause of the American debacle in Vietnam, where the insurgents were able to remain hidden much of the time, and had greater awareness of their opponents' plans and maneuvers. And attempts to find the guerrillas by "dangling the bait" with small Army and Marine patrols proved costly and frustrating. As Michael Maclear summarized, "On patrol, the GIs were inviting certain ambush."[46] This problem was never adequately solved in Vietnam, and recurred in Afghanistan and Iraq when insurgencies arose in these countries after American-led invasions.

In Iraq, though, General David Petraeus under-stood that failure to gather information about the insurgent networks was the critical deficiency that had so undermined the occupation forces' efforts during the first three years (2003–6) after the invasion. Given overall command there, Petraeus repeated techniques he had used in the Kurdish north – i.e., embedding with the locals rather than surging out patrols and raids from a handful of huge forward operating bases (FOBs). He knew that, as Victor Davis Hanson has summarized the Petraeus strategy, "He had to get his men outside the compounds, embed them within Iraqi communities, and develop human intelligence."[47] This was as much an information strategy as it was a military strategy. And the insurgents' information edge was soon blunted by the flow of intelligence about them that came from Iraqi locals who felt exploited by al Qaeda cadres. In less than a year, violence in Iraq dropped sharply. Where nearly 40,000 innocent Iraqis were being killed by terrorists each year before Petraeus and his emphasis on gaining an informational advantage, just a few thousand were lost to al Qaeda annually from 2008 until the American withdrawal at the end of 2011. When US forces returned in 2014, to fight the al Qaeda splinter group ISIS, the Petraeus model dominated. Only small numbers of Americans were sent; they embedded closely with indigenous forces, and decisively defeated ISIS.

But this aspect of cyberwar – controlling or "steering" the course of conflict by gaining and sustaining an information advantage – still has few adherents, and the dominant view of limiting cyberwar just to cyberspace-based operations prevails. It is a reason for failure to repeat the Petraeus approach in Afghanistan, where the reluctance to distribute small forces throughout the country among the friendly tribes – which worked so well there back in 2001 – allowed the Taliban insurgency to rise and expand. Sadly, even the very narrow, tech-only view of cyberwar has not been properly employed in Afghanistan, nor in broader counter-terrorism operations globally. In Afghanistan, the Taliban's command and control system, and movement of people, goods, weapons, and finances, all rely to some degree on communication systems – locally and with leaders in Pakistan – that are hackable. That they have *not* been compromised is proved by the growth of the insurgency. The same is true of worldwide counter-terror efforts; cyberspace is still a "virtual haven" for terror cells. Yes, they often rely on couriers. But the Taliban locally – as well as ISIS, al Qaeda, Hezbollah and a host of other dark groups who operate more widely – would be crippled if they were to lose faith in the security of their cyber/electronic communications. And if these systems were compromised secretly, *all* these groups would be destroyed. Even this narrower approach to cyberwar, if employed as the lead element in the counter-terror war, would prove decisive. As yet, this has not been the case. The world is much the worse for it.

Rise of the intelligent machines of war

Another technological aspect of cyberwar – an especially "cool" one – has to do with the rise of robots – or, more delicately put, artificial intelligence (AI). These machines, devices, and their software are the ultimate cyber tools, embodying the principles of control-through-feedback that Norbert Wiener envisioned. Back in the 1950s, he thought of the "human use of human beings." Today, we should be thinking about the "human use of artificial beings." In cyberspace, there is already much use of automation, by many countries, where bots have the authority to move swiftly on their own to counter attacks on information systems they are tasked with defending. The pace of cyberspace-based attacks is often too fast for humans to detect, track, and disrupt. On the more proactive side, there is widespread use of information-gathering AI "spiders" and other searchers – though the world's more democratic societies have strived to impose at least some limits on the use of such capabilities. And when it comes to employing bots in physical battle, those same liberal societies have regarded the matter as close to abhorrent, demanding almost always to keep a "human in the loop" for purposes of control. There is even an effort to ban the development of "killer robots," which has been championed at the United Nations and by many non-governmental organizations. Secretary-General António Guterres put the matter very starkly at a "web summit" held in late 2018:

> Machines that have the power and the discretion to take human lives are politically unacceptable, morally repugnant, and should be banned by international law.[48]

Guterres's speech buttressed the position of the 25 nations and the Holy See that had already signed on to the call to ban killer robots – and two more nations joined shortly after he spoke. However, as of this writing (2020), no NATO member states have supported such a prohibition on "Lethal Autonomous Weapons Systems" (LAWS); nor have the Russians. As to China, its position is to call for no first use of such weapons, but still to allow for their development and production. Interestingly, quite a few in the scientific and high-tech commercial sectors have embraced efforts to prevent the rise of military robotics. In 2015, 1,000 experts in AI signed an open letter expressing their opposition. At the same time, luminaries such as Stephen Hawking and Elon Musk took the position that the rise of robots, if allowed, could "spell the end of the human race."[49] This alarmist view has been articulated over the past several decades, the jumping-off point in popular culture probably being the 1984 film *The Terminator*. The *Matrix* movies and the re-booted television series *Battlestar Galactica* that came later both reinforced this trope, completely overshadowing Isaac Asimov's pacifistic "Laws of Robotics" – which he introduced in 1942, but about which even *he* wrote with ambivalence.

Around the same time that Arnold Schwarzenegger was first terrorizing humanity, scientist/novelist Michael Crichton was articulating the position that

> When the super-intelligent machine comes, we'll survive . . . The fear that in the coming years we will be replaced by our creations – that we will live with computers as our pets live with us – suggests an extraordinary lack of faith in human beings and their enterprise. . . . Our ancestors were threatened by trains and planes and electricity; we take these things for granted. Today we are threatened by computers; our descendants will take them for granted, too.[50]

Whether the AI alarmists are right will not be known for many decades – probably not for a few centuries. In the meantime, AI will continue to diffuse into virtually all aspects of life, and certainly into military and security affairs. Indeed, given the current trajectory of AI development, it is clear that armies, navies, and aerospace forces will soon be replete with robotics that sense, shoot – perhaps even do some strategizing.[51] But at present it seems clear that the patterns of development and diffusion are uneven, with the armed forces of authoritarian states embracing robotics far more actively and broadly than liberal, open societies. China has, in particular, jumped out well ahead in this new arms race, becoming, as one study has put it, an "AI superpower,"[52] while the United States – home to world-leading commercial, academic, and governmental research giants in the field – has lagged.

The reasons why the United States and other more open, market-oriented societies have fallen behind in the AI arms race will be explored in the following chapter. As will the policy paths that have led to the grave and ever-increasing vulnerability of individuals, commercial enterprises, government, the military, and other institutions that so powerfully affect society and security, especially in the world's democracies. It is ironic that the countries of the "free world" – such as it is – should be in dire straits in cyber-related matters, given that liberal polities were so successful over the past century in using advances in information technology to "hack" both fascism and communism. Literally. In World War II, for example, the Allied information edge – enabled by creation of the world's first true high-performance computers that fueled Britain's "Ultra" and the American "Magic" – had a profound impact on the outcome of that conflict. Both the German Enigma encryption system and the Imperial Japanese codes were hacked, enabling signal victories even when the material situation was sharply in favor of the aggressor, as at Midway in 1942. Hacks also played huge roles in the Battle of the Atlantic, at Normandy in 1944, and – by sharing informational coups with the Russians – on the all-important Eastern Front.[53] The failure of democracies today to craft Cyber-Age versions of Ultra and Magic courts disaster.

An era of social networks and "netwars"

Without question, cyberwarfare is on the rise throughout the world. Individuals, commercial companies, and institutions of all sorts are among the first to feel its sting, largely at the hands of those who click for pecuniary purposes. But the realms of "strategic crime" and subversion – primarily consisting of the theft of intellectual property in support of national aims, spying, and political warfare – are expanding at very rapid rates as well. All this is unfolding, undoubtedly, because defensive systems have proved so poor thus far. As to the more military aspects of cyberwar, the single-minded emphasis on developing this mode of operations in an inherently "strategic" manner has stunted the growth of a battle doctrine (*Bitskrieg*) implied and enabled by advances across a range of selected communications and information technologies. And when it comes to the rapid evolution of intelligent machines that lie at the heart of the world's latest arms race, there is a most curious phenomenon: authoritarian societies that have more centrally planned economies – supposedly inferior social designs – are well ahead of liberal, market-based nations with whom they are competing. Given that all forms of cyberwar – from the many abovementioned types of hacks to cybotage, political warfare, and new modes of battle – are and require "cool," it is somewhat surprising that those nations whose governance systems are considered balky, over-controlling, and sub-optimal are doing so well in the development of cool-war techniques. Most curious indeed.

There is one more important aspect of "cool" to consider in anticipation of future developments affecting society and security: Marshall McLuhan's. Half a century ago, McLuhan was contemplating "war and peace in the global village," and one of his keenest insights had to do with the notion of "cool media." The key distinguishing factor in his notion of "coolness" was counterintuitive: for McLuhan, the more the technology encouraged accessibility and mass engagement, the cooler it was. As he put it, "cool media are high in participation or completion by the audience."[54] Think of YouTube as an example of McLuhan's notion of coolness as measured in terms of levels of participatory "reach" and networked interactivity. In practical terms, McLuhan's notion of cool – he even wrote of the world moving toward a state of "cool war"[55] – means actualizing the potential of virtually every individual to achieve some form of power and influence, threatening the existing social order and power structures. It is interesting that McLuhan's prescient views coincided with the rise of massive social mobilization – for civil and voting rights, against the Vietnam War, to aid the Palestinians, protect the environment, and even more – as well as the rise of violent smaller movements such as the German Baader-Meinhof Gang, the American Students for a Democratic Society, and many others in his time. A wide range of today's terrorist groups fit this mold as well.

But it was the 1960s mass movements that truly foretold the rise and power of highly participatory – that is, "cool" – social networks such as Solidarity in

Poland, and the Czechs who engineered a "velvet revolution" in the 1980s. The later-on color revolutions, almost all successful, followed a similar pattern as well.[56] Even the less successful Arab Spring risings met McLuhan's definition of "cool." The same can be said for the waves of societal protest that raged around the world in 2019, from Latin American countries to Lebanon, Iraq, and Iran in the Middle East, and on to Hong Kong. All "cool," in McLuhan's sense, because of their high levels of engagement and interactive citizen/netizen participation. Essentially leaderless, they networked in ways allowing pursuit of a common goal absent central control. Kevin Kelly picked up on this theme neatly, noting the coolness, in practice, of digital media as a logical extension of Marshall McLuhan's concept.[57] David Ronfeldt and I used the term "social netwar" as our way to describe this subset of cyberwar, as manifested in civil conflicts within nations.[58] In these cases, the "cyber" nature of the battle is concentrated in the militants' use of information technologies to coordinate actions, strikes, gatherings, and in the governmental authorities' counter-efforts to limit networking – all too often ending in violent repression due to failure to disrupt the grassroots networks by other means.

Clearly, we are living in a cool war world whose evolution is propelled by information and communications technologies. It is a highly conflictual world, in that war – particularly cyberwar in its myriad forms – is no longer primarily the province of nations. Networks, even small ones – and even individuals – can now wage one or another form of cyberwar. Dark alliances may even arise between nations and networks – think of Hezbollah's close ties to Iran, for example, or the various hacker groups so friendly to Russia. The cyberwars waged in this new age of conflict can aim at innocent noncombatants and their homeland infra-structures – as strategic bombing has in earlier wars; attack commerce, much as pirates and other sea raiders have from time immemorial; and spark new modes of insurrection against authority. The fresh challenge of cyberwar is also driving yet another great transformation of so-called "conventional war," this time not based primarily on advances in weaponry, but more broadly on the notion of "steering" – remember that Greek root, *kybernan* – the course of a conflict by achieving an edge over the adversary in the gathering and management of timely, relevant information.

The good news is that cyberwar aims more at disruption than destruction, at achieving aims and goals at less cost, with less bloodshed, even in open warfare. The bad news is that there is a terrible imbalance between offense and defense today, with attackers having the edge, in and beyond cyberspace. How this has happened and how to mitigate this growing threat are issues considered next.

2

Pathways to Peril

In their thoughtful study of Information-Age conflict and security, Richard Clarke and Robert Knake – the former has served as a senior adviser to American presidents from both parties – have showed a great awareness of, and added meaningfully to, the discourse on the "offense–defense balance" as it has evolved in the realm of cyberwar. This balance – or "imbalance," as the case might be – has profound implications for the issues of war, peace, and deterrence that shape the quality of life in the international system. One of the most interesting aspects of their analysis is a comparison between the cyberwar-waging capabilities of leading nations – and some small, roguish states. Their considered judgments are eye-popping, the most troubling being that the world's military superpower, the United States, while fielding a top-flight offensive capability, has *the very worst defenses*. Russia, China, and Iran, for their parts, are rated as more evenly balanced, with mid-range offensive capabilities and among the very best-rated cyber defenses.[1] Poor American cybersecurity, in former

Chairman of the Joint Chiefs Admiral Michael Mullen's opinion, means that "cyber can bring us to our knees."[2]

The United States is hardly alone in its level of vulnerability to cyber attack. Indeed, most open societies – especially in the developed world, and particularly among its democracies – need to improve their own cyberspace-based defenses. One reason for their levels of vulnerability has to do simply with the nature of open societies: their technological advances make them more powerful and prosperous, but also much easier to strike at. Closing their societies, borders, and other aspects of ingress might improve security, but at great cost in economic terms and, perhaps more importantly, in relation to the self-identification of their people as "free." Writing near the end of the Cold War, journalist Norman Cousins thought retrospectively – and presciently too – about this enduring problem: "The dilemma is especially acute for free peoples. They have been vulnerable to aggressors in the past precisely because their freeness makes for openness."[3] An added challenge is faced by allies who attempt to integrate their defenses, but find that even one weak link can create overall cyber vulnerability. NATO members, for example, have had difficulty coordinating defenses, proving "insufficiently agile to contend with rapid and fundamental technological change" in cyber-related affairs, according to an influential Harvard University report.[4]

So, open societies are inherently more vulnerable to cyberspace-based disruptive attacks. Their penchant for crafting military alliances – a pattern authoritarians have tended to avoid since the collapse of the Warsaw Pact – only further complicates their security challenges. Then there is also the problem in alliances that they are often shaped by the possibly inappropriate preferences of a dominant member. To continue the example of NATO, in this instance the very strong American preference for taking the offensive in cyberspace has affected the cyber policies of other member states, given that they tend to "rely heavily on the United States and the discretion of U.S. commanders."[5] This is hardly good news, as it suggests that the serious American imbalance that has kept cyberspace-based defenses from being properly emphasized is diffusing broadly among the members of this key alliance. And beyond cyberspace, with regard to the broader notions of cyberwar, undue American influence on the way in which "cyber" ought to be understood – that is, just in terms of bits and bytes – may keep NATO from developing a holistic view of how advanced information technologies can be interwoven into overall military affairs. Thus, the implications for organizational redesign and doctrinal innovation – the very heart of *Bitskrieg* – may fail to be fully explored in Europe, mirroring the American failure.

Given that the United States serves as a kind of "strategic Patient Zero" when it comes to stunting the growth of the wide range of potential cyberwar capabilities, the reasons for American problems in this issue area are worth exploring. The market-driven economic structure of American society is at the top of this list. For decades now – ever since the personal computer's introduction – manufacturers have emphasized what consumers have prioritized: reasonable cost, memory/power, and speed, among other characteristics like weight, width, and aesthetic appeal. Consumers have not demanded security, so this feature has not been built in from the chip level on out. Software development suffered from similar neglect for quite a long time as well. It is a classic case of what economists call "market failure" to address an important issue. Only in the past decade has serious attention been paid to the need to manufacture secure products.[6] As to the Internet itself, the "information superhighway" was designed with too little attention given to security. Vinton Cerf, one of the Internet's founding fathers, admitted in an interview in 2015 – some five decades since its creation – "We didn't focus on how you could wreck this system intentionally."[7]

Needless to say, the consequences of this omission have deepened in seriousness in tandem with the tremendous expansion of the Internet, whose growth has retained the original design flaw that neglected security. It is a classic case of "path dependence," reflective of how difficult it can be to backtrack and redesign once a phenomenon has really taken off. To be sure, there have been voices of concern raised about the vulnerability that would come with connectivity. Among the first was Willis H. Ware of the RAND Corporation – one of my early mentors there. National-security expert Fred Kaplan summarized Ware's pioneering 1967 study of the new technology's susceptibilities: "once multiple users could access data from unprotected locations, anyone with certain skills could hack into the network – and after hacking into one part of the network, he could roam at will."[8] Ware's paper led to creation of a "Ware Panel" by the US Defense Science Board, whose 1970 report affirmed his concerns. But no real action ensued. The same held true three decades later when Dorothy and Peter Denning, two of the giants in computer science, brought together leaders in the field to try to deal with a by now "besieged" Internet. Still, no effective policies emerged.[9]

Given that "the market" was not, of its own volition, going to address this problem, computers and their connectivity remained highly vulnerable to exploitation and disruption. As to government, in its regulatory capacity, "securing cyberspace" proved a double-edged

concept. While authoritarian states and other less free
polities were able to impose controls on access and
monitor systems in place with relative ease – China and
Singapore providing the archetypal examples – democracies had troubles from the outset in their efforts to
establish and sustain regulatory roles in cyberspace.
Once again, the United States was exemplary of this
problem. Early on, this took the form of a "data
encryption standard" (DES) limited to a quite weak
56-bit key – when 128 was recommended by experts
in the field. Given that each time a single bit is
removed from key length it cuts the level of effort
of any codebreaker *in half*, a 56-bit key was, in
technical terms, an affront to the notion of security. But
the American intelligence agencies – in particular, the
National Security Agency – and the law enforcement
community were very reluctant to allow restrictions
of any sort to be placed on their capabilities to access
electronic communications. As Steven Levy observed,

> while an ideal code for users was the strongest one
> possible, the ideal code for the NSA's purposes would
> be one that was too powerful for criminals and other
> foes to break, but just weak enough to be broken by the
> billions of subterranean cycles at Fort Meade.[10]

Needless to say, the 56-bit key was hardly "too
powerful" to keep malefactors out. And when experts
in the private sector began to develop strong encryption
as a product that could be distributed – or even
marketed – the US government had to give ground
and allow longer-bit keys. But there was to be a catch:
stronger security was to be accompanied by the government's ability to intrude via a so-called "Clipper Chip,"
an encryption device intended to secure communications,
but which had a "backdoor" enabling government to

access and decode all voice and data transmissions. This was an initiative that many civil society actors, such as the Electronic Privacy Information Center and the Electronic Frontier Foundation – and even some in the Department of Defense – found very deeply troubling.[11] The chip died an unquiet death in 1996, thanks in part to a strong bipartisan critique of it spearheaded by Senators John Ashcroft and John Kerry. Their spirited defense of privacy rights has echoed ever since among conservatives and liberals alike – both in the United States and in other democracies. The European Union, in particular, has taken a very strong stand in favor of "the legitimate security interests of users." Britain, however, still desires "uninhibited access by national authorities to encrypted messages."[12]

Despite the seeming victory of the socio-political coalition in favor of "giving strong encryption to the people," some parts of the United States government continued, quietly, with efforts to create a form of oversight of all cyber communications. Known by various codenames, like "Topsail" and "Genoa" – and the much more ominous-sounding "Total Information Awareness" – these disparate initiatives did make some serious headway in monitoring. And then the 9/11 terrorist attacks on America in 2001 provided additional justification for their continuance, and the development of other initiatives, despite the civil liberties concerns being raised, in and outside of government. Thus, counter-terrorism efforts did indeed allow the security community greater freedom to act. Too much freedom, sparking resistance and an increasing desire to "out" these over-aggressive monitoring methods – such as "XKeyscore" and other tools detailed in 2013 when Edward Snowden made his revelations about shady deals with high-tech companies and fiber optic cable-tapping capabilities. Both Wikileaks and *The Guardian* played major roles in publicizing these massive data grabs, creating a firestorm in the global discourse about the role that governments in supposedly free societies can and should play in securing – but also in exploiting – private communications for ostensibly "higher" national-security purposes.[13]

The sheer amount of data captured by government monitoring systems that Snowden revealed – he leaked perhaps as many as 2,000,000 US files, and fewer but still significant numbers of British and Australian files – was shocking. Snowden himself became a fugitive, and at this writing (2020) is still sheltered by Russia. A traitor to some, whistleblower to others, he has both sparked an important debate and done serious damage to the American intelligence-gathering processes.

Another example of strong opposition to the government's intrusion into individual privacy arose when Apple chief executive Tim Cook refused to assist the FBI in unlocking the iPhone of Syed Farook, perpetrator of a domestic terrorist attack that took place in San Bernardino, California, in 2016. Farook and his wife – she was in on the plot – were killed in a shootout; the FBI wanted to glean what information they could from the retrieved iPhone. But they could not break its four-digit password without triggering the data erasure that would ensue after ten unsuccessful tries. So, the FBI asked Cook to help. He refused, noting that "at stake is the data security of hundreds of millions of law-abiding people and setting a dangerous precedent that threatens everyone's civil liberties."[14]

In the event, the FBI circumvented what would undoubtedly have been a bitter, protracted court battle by hiring hackers who figured out how to avoid the data erasure feature.[15] But this turned out to be something of a pyrrhic victory, as the imbroglio with the government prompted Apple to make further security improvements to its iPhone. Thus, Apple's refusal to break into the devices of the Saudi officer who perpetrated the 2019 terrorist attack at the Pensacola naval air station was significantly buttressed by this improved level of security. About this incident, Apple took the position that "calls for guaranteed-access mechanisms in encryption were misguided," and reaffirmed its belief that "encryption is vital to protecting our country and our users' data."[16]

The American government's continuing efforts to gain untrammeled access to strongly encrypted personal data – a preference shared by many others, in both "free" and authoritarian societies – as well as to maintain a vigorous general surveillance program, have kindled much hostility among information technology experts more broadly, with some in this community even vowing publicly that in the future they would demur when asked to undertake *any* national-security-related work.

One of the more dramatic examples of this growing antipathy came in 2018 – after the San Bernardino iPhone incident, but before the dispute over the phones of the Pensacola terrorist – when 3,000 Google employees signed a statement demanding that their company leave the Pentagon's "Project Maven," an effort to optimize the utility of drone video feeds for targeting purposes using the latest advances in artificial intelligence, when the initial contract was up.[17] One can, and probably should, be open to a debate about the merits of top experts in a key technology sector "opting out" of the national defense. A troubling example, though, would be to think of the leading scientists of the Allies refusing to work on the Manhattan Project during World War II. And it is particularly vexing today to think of confronting the challenge of cyberwar without the active support – particularly in "free" societies – of the people most qualified to meet and master this challenge.

So, in addition to the "market failure" to address cybersecurity at the manufactured-product level, there has also been, particularly in the world's more liberal polities, the inability of these governments to address this issue area adequately in their role as regulators. The free-wheeling "invisible hand" of the market may have proved unable to deal effectively with the most pernicious threats to cybersecurity; but the visible hand of government – particularly of democratic governance – has failed as well. The problem for liberal governments has been the official ambivalence created by the perceived dual need to protect the people while at the same time retaining a right to intrude upon their privacy for national-security purposes.

In addition to these economic and political difficulties that stand in the way of good cybersecurity, there is also what I see to be a major flaw in the engineered design of cybersecurity for information and other infrastructures. Think telecommunications, power grids, pipelines, and more. Simply put, in developed countries, much infrastructure has been in place since before the rise of cyberspace. These pre-cyber systems, first built without ubiquitous connectivity in mind, are being linked to the Net and the Web. This makes them vulnerable. How vulnerable? In the case of the United States (yet again), the risk level is extremely high. According to a confidential letter sent to a member of the House of Representatives in 2010, signed by a bipartisan group of former secretaries of defense and directors of the CIA:

> Virtually all of our civilian critical infrastructure – including telecommunications, water, sanitation,

transportation, and healthcare – depends on the electric grid. The grid is extremely vulnerable to disruption by a cyber- or other attack. Our adversaries already have the capability to carry out such an attack. The consequences of a large-scale attack on the U.S. grid would be catastrophic for our national security and economy . . . Under current conditions, timely recon-struction of the grid following a carefully targeted attack, if particular equipment is destroyed, would be impossible.[18]

The inherent weakness associated with connecting an older set of systems to the latest information and communications technologies – now at the "5G" level, with China's Huawei in a leading role – was compounded long ago by the US government's decision to deregulate "power" under the terms of the National Energy Policy Act passed in 1992. Since then, rather than have a small number of large providers, the highly networked electrical power grid has consisted of a *few thousand companies* of widely varying sizes. The implication of this complexity is that, as Ted Koppel has noted: "The very structure that keeps electricity flowing . . . depends absolutely on computerized systems designed to maintain perfect balance between supply and demand . . . the Internet provides the instant access to the computerized systems that maintain that equilibrium."[19] Thus, the interconnectivity of this largely de-regulated, privately owned infrastructure means that a weakness anywhere can lead to serious disruption everywhere. It puts a very high premium on strong cybersecurity. Yet the principal means by which defenses have been pursued – within and *beyond* the realm of infrastructure – have proved inadequate, based on the record of costly intrusions that have bedeviled protective efforts for decades.

Cybersecurity strategy needs retooling

Most cyber defenses have long consisted of: (1) "firewalls" that check all incoming or outgoing messages to ensure they meet security criteria; and (2) "anti-virals" designed to scan for and remove computer viruses. Firewalls, even "next-generation" ones featuring "deep packet inspection," are, in the considered view of leading security experts, "nothing more than a filter . . . [that] analyzes what goes through against a rule set, according to specific sets of criteria."[20] Master hackers have repeatedly shown me how they can "walk through" firewalls by presenting inputs that meet all security criteria while at the same time concealing the elements they wish to insert into a system. As to anti-virals, these can only screen out or de-bug malicious software of which they are already aware. As one commentator has put it, four new strains emerge, worldwide, *every second*; and malware "hasn't only proliferated; it has evolved to better evade detection."[21]

If neither firewalls nor anti-virals can stop intrusive cyber onslaughts, why is it that the cybersecurity industry is dominated by them? Part of their appeal, no doubt, is metaphorical. Customers / system users can easily grasp the notion of a virtual wall because we are all familiar with physical walls – we live and work within them, and are kept safe and comforted by them. Similarly, we are all familiar with the benefits of vaccines, and of our own immune systems that help cope with biological viruses. But these metaphors – like all metaphors – have limits; and inappropriate application of them can lead to costly errors. When it comes to the need to secure cyberspace – for individuals, commercial firms, institutional entities, government, and the military – it is high time to move away from too-convenient metaphors and get back to the most enduring truth about how to protect information: *encode* it. As Peter Singer and Allan Friedman have put the matter, so clearly and compellingly, "if you cannot prevent attackers from accessing the data, you *can* limit their ability to understand the data through encryption."[22]

Julius Caesar, one of history's most famous adventurer-conquerors, began using a very basic letter substitution code – plaintext "a" became "D," b = E, c = F, etc. – in his dispatches from Gaul, an innovation that, as David Kahn noted, "impressed his name permanently into cryptology."[23] Polybius, less famously, preceded Caesar with a number–letter substitution system. Such methods have characterized encoding for millennia.

Of course, the level of sophistication of codes has evolved over these many centuries; but code-making has been in an action–reaction cycle with codebreakers virtually the whole time. And when Alan Turing and the other "boffins" at Bletchley Park built the first high-performance computer during World War II, even the German Enigma encoding machine – it ultimately had four alphabetic rotors that created 456,976 possibilities per keystroke[24] – fell prey to decryption. In recent decades, though, advances in cryptography have made it possible to work and communicate comfortably with very-long-bit key lengths, giving a real and durable advantage to code-makers. This makes it even more puzzling that ubiquitous use of strong encryption has not been the norm in the product market; nor has it been the goal of governments – all too many governments – in their regulatory roles. Instead, Maginot-Line-like thinking has prevailed, broadly diffusing throughout the world vast numbers of brittle firewalls that, when penetrated, allow hackers to roam widely, raiding and plundering at will. The simple alternative to Maginot Lines is to "imagine no lines," preparing instead for inevitable intrusions, but yielding little to interlopers who may make their way into a system.

Embracing the ubiquitous use of strong encryption would indeed enable sharp, immediate improvements in cybersecurity, for individuals and institutions, commerce and governance, and for civil society and the military. And this opportunity should, unquestionably, be seized. But the enduring duel between code-makers and code-breakers will go on; strong encryption's current edge will be challenged, a development for which preparation should be made *now*. We already know that the most potent threat to secure codes, currently just a bit (no pun) over the technological horizon, will come from quantum computing, whose power will arise from going immeasurably far beyond the capacity of the traditional computer chip by taking the capacity to create the zeros and ones of binary code down to the subatomic level. The building of the first high-performance computer at Bletchley Park is an accomplishment that will pale in comparison to the potential of these new "qbits." In one of the first successful tests of quantum computing power, the Google "Sycamore" machine broke a code that would have taken a current-era supercomputer thousands of years to solve. This successful test has been disputed by Google's competitors – all striving to make quantum computing advances of their own. But indications are that qbits herald what promises to be a period of revolutionary change in code-breaking capacities.[25]

For all its potential, though, quantum computing should not be seen as bringing a definitive conclusion to the ages-old rivalry between code-makers and code-breakers in favor of the latter. Secure defenses are still going to be possible, as qbits can be used to create keys of exceptional length that will greatly complicate the decoding process. Indeed, there is a whole field of inquiry under way that aims at how to build "quantum-safe" encryption.[26] In addition, newly strengthened encryption can be further reinforced by skillful employment of Cloud computing, the use of remote servers on the Internet to store and process data. Imagine taking some particular body of important data, strongly encrypting it, then breaking that data into pieces and parceling it out among a number of remote servers. This poses a much harder task for the hacker who, if the data were centrally held, would simply have to breach a firewall. As I have said to colleagues in the defense community over the years, "Data at rest are data at risk." What sits on one's own system already has a bull's eye on it. Dispersal is the *sine qua non* of data security. The Pentagon finally accepted this view in 2019, awarding a Cloud-computing contract to Microsoft – contested by Amazon – for $10 billion.[27]

Despite progressive thinking about shifting cybersecurity toward greater reliance on strong encryption and Cloud computing, the situation remains perilous. For decades, market forces did not drive the IT industry to make very secure products – true as well of the manufacturers of a range of products now reachable via the Internet of Things. And old infrastructure, "hotwired" to the Net and the Web, is poorly engineered for security against advanced hacking techniques. Furthermore, the business model of the cybersecurity sector, so committed to firewalls and anti-viral software, has slowed progress toward the goals of making ubiquitous use of strong encryption and Cloud computing.

The vulnerabilities mentioned in this and the preceding chapter, and the reasons why proper responses have not arisen to mitigate cyber threats, are causes for great concern. The steady streams of widely publicized and costly data breaches that have led to the loss of highly valuable intellectual property, and the holding for ransom of operationally important information from commercial and governmental entities – and sometimes even affected the reliability of military systems – should have prompted sharp remedial action by now. That they have not is an indictment of the governmental and commercial sectors, especially in the world's more open societies where the political opposition to regulation comes from liberals *and* conservatives, and where the cybersecurity business sector is heavily invested in – therefore, reluctant to give up – tools and methods that are already highly permeable, even in the face of attacks by only modestly skilled hackers.

What about cyberterrorism?

For all the grave concerns that bedevil efforts to improve cybersecurity, there is a curious area in which an eerie near-silence prevails: terrorism. Why? For terrorist networks, crafting a truly serious capability to mount cyber attacks would seem a most attractive goal. At low risk, they could be able to engage in costly disruption – a reasonable course change after many decades of failing to achieve their aims by means of occasional acts of violence perpetrated against innocents. If one counts the modern era of terrorism as arising, for the most part, in the wake of the Irish Troubles and Palestinian efforts to achieve statehood – both of which began in earnest in the late 1960s – it seems, as Conor Gearty noted, "terrorism has achieved little of any consequence. No government has fallen because of its attacks, comparatively few casualties have been sustained, and no terrorist group has achieved anything more than a fraction of its long-term aims."[28]

Gearty's assertion, made in 1991, is still true, even when al Qaeda's attacks on America in 2001 – and violence perpetrated by its affiliates and imitators there-after – are factored in. However, there are other ways to think about terrorism's impact: in terms of its ability to gain wide attention, and as a means of provoking costly, counter-productive over-reactions. For example, Paul Wilkinson observes that terrorism "has an impressive record in gaining such things as massive world-wide publicity."[29] And, in terms of provoking violent over-reaction, as Richard English has thoughtfully argued, "terrorists have recognized the great value to their cause of provoking states into such counter-productive militarization, with the spectacular backfiring of such policies often having a long-term effect."[30] The chronic American troubles in Afghanistan and Iraq in the years since the invasions of these sad lands – in 2001 and 2003, respectively – bear out English's point. Thus, if attention-getting and provocation are terrorist goals, it would certainly seem that cyberterror would also have value as an added tool, for both purposes. It also has the side benefits that it doesn't require suicide bombing, and hard-to-find hackers are less vulnerable to retali-atory commando raids.

Cyberterror can work on three main levels: (1) as a means of waging political warfare and propagan-dizing in ways that discomfit the enemy and aid in gaining popular support, and recruits, from among its target audiences; (2) for purposes of mounting virtual hit-and-run raids, like the varied attacks perpetrated against Saudi Arabian oil and other infrastructures – allegedly by Iranian or Iran-allied hackers; and (3) with "mass disruption" in mind, to such a crippling degree, as Walter Laqueur once pointed out, that cyberterror "exposes enormous vital areas of national life to mischief or sabotage by any computer hacker, and concerted sabotage could render a country unable to function."[31] David Sanger has observed that nation-states are using cyber for all the above reasons;[32] but why have terrorist networks limited themselves to the first of these levels of activity, focusing on propaganda functions? They have done little along the lines of infrastructure strikes, and hardly any more in the realm of small-scale disruptive attacks. Thomas Chen sums the situation up succinctly: "No serious cyberterrorism attacks have occurred."[33]

There has been serious attention given to the potential for cyberterror – across much of the developed world – since before 9/11. One of the most important early efforts to understand and predict the developmental path of this new threat of "mass disruption" came from the Marsh Commission Report, a broad study of infrastructure vulnerability ordered by American President Bill Clinton and released publicly in 1997. The report, produced by a team of 20 commissioners and an even larger staff, judged virtual terrorism as having very serious potential, so much so that "the Commission focused more on cyber issues than physical issues."[34] However, there were dissents offered up as well. For example, an official report on cyberterror sponsored by the Defense Intelligence Agency – conducted by a far smaller team than Marsh's – argued in its Foreword:

> Our view is not that cyberterror will fail to emerge as a serious threat. Rather, we see that the barriers to entry, for any capability beyond annoying hacks, are quite high; and that terrorists generally have neither the wherewithal nor the human capital needed to mount cyberterror operations on a meaningful level. Thus, because of the difficult technical path that must still be followed, cyberterror is not a threat. At least not yet, and not for a while.[35]

What was asserted back then is still the case, especially with regard to the potential of networks of non-state-affiliated terrorists to mount cyber attacks of a serious nature. Why is this judgment about the prospects for cyberterror still valid? There are two sets of reasons: one psychological, the other practical. In terms of the "terrorist mind," there is a significant body of study, going back many decades, that suggests terrorists believe more in the power of physical violence against innocent people to instill broad fears in others and gain their compliance, than in the value of any other type of action. As Palestinian terrorist Bassam Abu Sharif put the matter back in the 1970s, "I am committed to killing to save my people."[36] Along with such an externally oriented, self-described altruistic/strategic mindset, there is also in some cases an inward-oriented psychological sense of fulfillment achieved by bloody violence – even of the suicidal sort – that cannot be experienced by other means. This inner-directed form of self-satisfaction is often tied to belief, on the terrorist's part, in being a soldier in a "cosmic war" that has apocalyptic implications – and may lead to the pursuit of nuclear and other weapons of mass destruction.[37] Cyber capabilities do not meet this need.

In addition to the "psychological barrier to entry," there is also a more practically oriented reason that may help to provide an explanation for why cyberterror has not thrived. It has to do with the very nettlesome problem of needing to possess a high level of skill in the complex workings of advanced information technology – sufficiently high to enable the terrorist to know where and how to strike to achieve some degree of "mass disruption." Where is such a capability to come from? One straightforward solution would seem to be outsourcing. To be sure, there are many hackers for hire, in increasing numbers around the world – from lone, disaffected computer scientists to those who have been co-opted or groomed by criminal organizations, and even some who have broken with the nation-states for whom they had been working. The key problem with outsourcing a cyber capability is that such mercenaries may lack a mindset that melds well with the true believers in a terrorist group. This may spark mistrust, planting the seed that the hacker might actually be an infiltrator whose aim is to learn just enough about the network to illuminate its members, steal its money, and then direct counter-terrorist forces' missile strikes and commando raids. No, cyber mercenaries are not likely to be sought to give a terrorist group the capability to attack and disrupt advanced information systems. The risks are simply too high.[38]

To all these impediments, psychological and practical, to terrorist development of a robust capacity for engaging in cyberterror, can also be added the unlikelihood that a nation-state sponsor might provide extremist networks with sophisticated cyber weaponry. A state actor would, in almost all cases – the Iran–Hezbollah relationship is perhaps the one nation–network tie that might serve as an exception – have to worry about the reliability of its secret non-state partner. What if the network were to turn on its nation-state ally? Just as bad would be a situation in which the terrorists in question were tracked down or infiltrated, the link to the state sponsor substantiated forensically. Not only would the cyber weaponry involved be compromised – defenses would immediately be upgraded to cope with the types of threats they posed – but the state sponsor would be subject to intense international opprobrium. It is far more likely that nation-state actors will grow their own hacker corps, and bring any cyber mercenaries they do recruit within their own borders – as these "clickers for hire" can mount their malicious acts from anywhere, and might as well be kept under close control. It is hardly surprising that the Internet Research Agency, the "Trolls from Olgino" – alleged to be among Russia's principal cyber mischief-making assets – is quartered and kept quite securely in St. Petersburg.[39]

Despite all these reasons why there have been so few, if any, acts of cyberterror, there may still be a long-term, internally driven approach for terrorists to take in pursuit of this path. It has to do with their deepening understanding that social media can be employed to mobilize, recruit, and incite individuals to commit acts of terror. This view has taken on much significance among Muslims with sophisticated computer skills who have joined the cause of the "virtual media jihad." Muhammad bin Ahmad al-Salim, one of the leading voices in this discourse, has labeled the practice of social media radicalization "a blessed field which contains much benefit."[40] Maybe the skills needed to elude those who would shut down cyber jihadis will eventually lead to development of sufficient craft to begin engaging in truly disruptive and destructive cyber attacks. A last – and very long-term – possibility might be to recruit a youth who has strong kinship ties, religious devotion, and perhaps some sense of family obligation, then send him (or her) to school to study computer science in any of a number of countries where a top-flight computer science education is to be had. Such a process would likely take a decade from the time the recruit began these studies, but identification and initial solicitation would have to start many years earlier.

These last two paths to terrorist acquisition of truly disruptive cyber capabilities both require much time and patience, and in the case of sending a selected recruit off to study, there is the added factor of possible discovery or disillusionment. If the recruit were uncovered and then monitored, for years, by a counter-terrorist agency, the entire terrorist organization might end up being compromised. A similar risk would arise if the recruit were to have a change of heart about becoming a terrorist. And the notion of having several such candidates going through university and graduate school to gain high-level cyber skills, in the hope that one or two might make it, increases the catastrophic risks associated with the discovery or disillusionment of *any* of them.

It is imperative to note at this point that not all cyberterror should be viewed as Islamic in origin or motivation. Nor should a capacity for virtual mass disruption be associated only with bits and bytes. It is not my intent to provide guidance to potential cyberter-rorists, but those who would thwart them must also realize that major disruptive effects can be achieved against information systems and infrastructures with explosives, strong magnets, and microwave emissions. The US Department of State formally recognizes attacks against physical structures as terrorism; the Colombian FARC rebels for years engaged in attacks on oil pipelines for exactly such purposes.

But the very first known act of physical cyberterror, which was perpetrated perhaps somewhat unwit-tingly, occurred during the Vietnam War in 1972 when the American dissident Bill Ayers set off a bomb in a Pentagon lavatory. As he recalled in his memoir, pipes broke and "water plunged [to the floor] below and knocked out their computers for a time, disrupting the air war."[41] A decade later, an act thought to be state-sponsored cyberterror/cybotage – but which is *still* not confirmed – saw an alleged CIA plot succeed by "duping Moscow into stealing booby-trapped software [that] triggered a huge explosion in a Siberian gas pipeline."[42] More recently, the vulnerability of critical power infrastructure to low-tech physical attack was demonstrated in 2013 in California's Bay Area when rifle shots fired by a team, operating in a synchronized manner, hit fifteen transformers crucial to keeping the juice flowing to much of Silicon Valley. The attacks could have had grave consequences had damage been worse, as replacement would have required importing specialized equipment and expertise, likely taking many months to arrange.[43] The cost of this disruption would have been enormous.

And this "Metcalf Sniper Incident" – so named because it was Pacific Gas & Electric's Metcalf Transmission Substation that was hit – may have been just a dry-run test of this mode of cyberwarfare, featuring physical attacks aimed at information infrastructural targets. A similar incident occurred in Utah in 2016, when a lone sniper disabled a substation of that state's Garkane Energy Cooperative, causing a day-long power outage. As one technical analyst noted, this incident was "reminiscent of an attack on a Pacific Gas and Electric substation in 2013" – though the perpetrator in Utah succeeded this time, causing a service disruption that affected over 10,000 local residents. The Garkane event is, as the analyst concluded, "a reminder that large portions of the United States' grid remain vulnerable to attack, potentially from either cyber intrusions or [by] being physically disabled."[44] To my mind, either option qualifies as cyberwarfare. It's a "big tent."

Will nations engage in "cybotage"?

Non-state terrorist and/or militant organizations will likely have difficulty attaining the high levels of technical skill needed to mount sophisticated cyber attacks – and may have psychological preferences for killing, rather than "clicking," or shooting at or blowing up targets other than people. But their "failure to bark" in the cyberterrorist night only begs a question: why is it that nation-states don't engage in such acts on their own, or by using closely controlled and monitored mercenaries and hackers? After all, these actions can be undertaken clandestinely. And, if discovered, there is always the option to issue a bald-faced denial, even when confronted with evidence of one's misdeeds. Escalation to open conflict is unlikely. This was truly the case during the Cold War when Moscow acted as the hub of a terrorist network that committed or orchestrated a range of varied types of attacks, including bombings and assassinations. As Claire Sterling observed in her classic *The Terror Network*, initially "the Kremlin took an avuncular interest in terrorist 'adventurers' of every alarming shade." Soviet involvement in such ventures grew into a more activist, if still covert, role during the 1970s and early 1980s. It was a seemingly very low-risk, high-return investment in mayhem-making.[45] Pulitzer-Prize-winning journalist Sanche de Gramont saw the creation of such networks as having links to espionage as well, which, combined with dark deeds, had the ability to "engulf billions of dollars, jeopardize the lives of many men, and add to international tension."[46]

Today, in this "cool war" era, the Russians seem content for the most part to engage in acts of political warfare in cyberspace. But why wouldn't they want to commit or foment much more physi- cally disruptive – or even destructive – covert cyber actions? A similar question may be asked of the Chinese. One of the leading teams of Western cyber strategists contends that Beijing's preference, above all, is for the theft of intellectual property, rather than for overtly disruptive or destructive acts.[47] Such restraint is puzzling, given the great – and growing – vulnerabilities of most open societies, whose governments tend to be severely hog-tied by both liberals and conservatives

concerned about privacy rights, making regulatory and/
or legislative fixes difficult, indeed near-impossible, to
enact. Their free markets have failed to produce truly
secure products, because the huge masses of poorly
informed consumers have not demanded them. And
the business model for cybersecurity that *has* emerged
is based on the faulty paradigms of "walls" and "anti-
virals." The former concept is, as mentioned earlier,
an artifact of classic linear strategic thinking. The
latter notion, so generally soothing to governmental,
commercial, and institutional actors, as well as to
individuals, is perhaps even more dangerous. For if an
attacking virus is unfamiliar to a targeted system, it will
be able to run through its victims like an epidemic.

The lethality of viruses is a very well-known physical
phenomenon that affects a wide range of living things.
Jared Diamond has observed this vulnerability as it
manifested among humans – especially during the great
age of oceanic discovery and conquest several centuries
ago – becoming something like a weapon of mass
destruction that aimed at varied indigenous peoples
whose immune systems proved utterly unable to deal
with the new germs brought to them by European
explorer/conquerors.[48] Most recently, the COVID-19
pandemic has showed that, even in this age of very
advanced medical science, a new pathogen for which
there are no existing immunities can have absolutely
mass-disruptive social and economic effects.

The same pattern has held true in cyberspace, from
the early "Morris Worm" incident in 1988, which shut
down a large portion of the Internet, to the more recent
virus that came out of Ukraine in 2017 and spread
swiftly and widely throughout the world. Where the
Morris matter grew from a student's experimentation
gone awry, the more recent incident, clearly malicious
in intent, had a deeply disturbing new feature. It was

an apparent retooling and repurposing of a secret American cyber weapon that had somehow ended up "in the wild" – and clearly in the wrong hands. The somewhat modified "Eternal Blue" virus very quickly disrupted movements of goods at over 70 ports, from Mumbai to Los Angeles. Other types of commercial activity were disrupted as well, with Federal Express among the prominent victims of this attack. Overall, tens of thousands of computer systems were also taken down – a very significant portion of them, beyond Ukraine, in Italy.[49] The point here is that, if the virtual pathogen is new, or even just a modestly changed version of an older one, its disruptive power can be immense. And exceptionally costly.

In such a state of affairs, one might ask, "Why aren't nation-states waging vigorous, if covert, cyberwars right now?" One obvious explanation is that cyber aggressors are deterred from acting out of fear of retaliation if their veils of anonymity were pierced by increasingly sophisticated forensic capabilities. This in turn might spark more vigorous responses to ongoing "strategic crimes" aimed at stealing vital intellectual property (think China), or to cyberspace-based political warfare (think Russia). These are at present still low-risk, high-return activities that perpetrators would surely be loath to have to curtail in any way. Escalating, by engaging in mass-disruptive acts, might well turn a profitable cool war hot, at the cost of making any further gains via strategic crime and political warfare.

There is another important reason why we have seen little more than exploratory and experimental elements of tactical and strategic cyberwar, as in the Russian, or "pro-Russian," uses of cyber attacks in Estonia (2007), Georgia (2008), and Ukraine (since 2014). To use very advanced cyber tools capable of achieving serious disruptive effects during a (relatively) more peaceful time – or in the context of a lower-intensity conflict – could mean that these same tools would be unavailable when a larger war came along. Cyber weaponry of the most precise, sophisticated sort – like Stuxnet, which was designed to attack a specific type of software used in Iranian centrifuges – takes great effort to design, test, and develop. Then, once used, it identifies both itself *and* the particular vulnerability of the system that it has attacked, making it hard to use the same cyber weapon again. In this sense, modern cyber weaponry has a "wasting asset" quality; whatever the size of one's arsenal of such attack tools, the use of any diminishes the total available until new malware is developed. For it is highly unlikely that a specific cyber weapon, once used, will succeed a second time. To be sure, there can be efforts to retool older "exploits" so as to make them usable again. But the thoughtful defender has this possibility in mind as well, and prepares for such variants. Thus, to conduct cyberwar, the need is not for large arsenals of the same weapons, but rather for a range of new *types* of weapons.

This problem of the constant need for variety in a cyber arsenal may provide much of the explanation for why there has been so little strategic – and tactical – cyberwar to date. It makes poor sense in a period of peace – say, between two great powers – for one to engage in strategic attacks upon the critical infrastructure of the other. The disruptions will be fixed, the victims of the attack will have deeper understanding of their vulnerabilities, and the attacker will have lost the use of an important cyber-attack tool. Much better to wait until an actual war is under way, then, amid the hurly-burly of an ongoing conflict, cause mass disruption. Perhaps this is one reason why Presidents Obama and Xi, at a meeting in 2015, discussed the possibility of an agreement under whose terms the United States and

China would refrain from attacking the other's infra-structure by cyber means *during peacetime*.[50] A formal accord was not reached; but this would have been a good example of acting in the interest of maintaining the size of, and operational control over, each country's cyber arsenals. The overture that President Obama made constituted an effort to begin the process of pursuing "behavior-based" arms control – something for which I lobbied when on a small team he tasked with finding "new directions for defense." Prospects for cyber arms control will be discussed in detail in Chapter 4.

This problem of "use-and-lose" affects cyber weapons in all their contemplated strategic roles, creating a dynamic wherein their employment limits future viability. This problem also applies to tactical battlefield uses as well; what works to disrupt commu-nications, to locate an artillery battery, etc., on one occasion, or even a few, might be quickly countered once detected (as was the case with pro-Russian forces' phone hacks that were locating Ukrainian units with GPS-level precision – for a while). This problem of cyber weapons having a "wasting asset" quality has been very thoughtfully examined by Robert Axelrod and Rumen Iliev in a breakthrough study they conducted for the National Academies of Science.[51] They recog-nized the different levels of complexity – from simple to sophisticated – of the various types of cyber weapons, then related them to the "stakes" (i.e., low, medium, or high) that were involved in any situation where the use of cyber weapons was contemplated. To this mix, they added a way to calculate the range of other important factors, like the risk over time of the detection of a secretly implanted cyber exploit before it could be used. Overall, Axelrod and Iliev were able to create an analytic framework for identifying conditions under which one might use high-value, perhaps irreplaceable, cyber weapons; in short, it would have to be in high-stakes situations. Like hot, shooting wars.

This begs the question "Who will be doing the shooting – or rather, the clicking – in the cyberwars of the future?" Most advanced militaries, across many countries, are trying to develop cyber cadres capable of these sorts of operations. But this takes time, especially in the more democratic countries that tend to require cyber operators who wear the uniform to meet mental and physical standards, and to be able to be vetted sufficiently to be granted high-level clearances. In the United States, for example, clearance processes can take many months, sometimes longer. As to the choice to use civilian contractors, again the more liberal societies tend to apply standards that prevent quick recruitment – often precluding even the possibility of recruitment, as I have found more than once when trying to bring a master hacker "into the fold." Authoritarian countries – Russia, China, and North Korea, to name a few – have the edge here in hacker recruitment, as they are more willing to reach out to so-called "black hat" hackers and bring them on board. These desperadoes are able quickly to raise the quality and speed of development of the cyber forces of the nations for whom they are working, whose governments have less fear of this sort of recruitment than terrorists do. Thus, crack cyber teams are formed, such as China's Unit 61398, five of whose officers were indicted by the United States Department of Justice in 2014 for their hacks – which 61398 continues to this day.

Clearly, the American legal action is futile. Indictments are not going to impede the "organizational race" – which goes on alongside the arms race to craft malware – to build formal cyber cadres in a number of the militaries of more authoritarian nation-states. Even

worse, democratic states all too often have developed
extremely hostile relations with hacker communities.
They are particularly bad in the United States, where
relatively harmless hacks can land an individual in
deep trouble with the law. The very saddest example is
of Aaron Swartz, a genius programmer who helped to
develop the web feed RSS ("really simple syndication")
and co-founded Reddit, one of the leading social news
sites. Among other aims, Swartz wanted to see that
academic journal articles were made more widely and
easily available. So, he hacked an MIT network to get
at the largest archive and, when detected in 2011, was
arrested and brought up on a range of charges under the
Computer Fraud and Abuse Act. A period of increasingly testy negotiations around a plea bargain ended
with the government refusing to deal. Two days later,
Swartz committed suicide.[52] This tragedy grew from the
collision between a reasonable desire to make scholarly
studies widely available and proprietary rules about
information control and dissemination – which then
escalated due to an apparent belief that harsh action
against hackers could deter them.

Another troubling case is that of Gary McKinnon, an
autistic Scottish hacker who was apparently interested
in learning "the truth" about UFOs and anti-gravity
technology supposedly obtained by reverse engineering
materials retrieved from the crash sites of alien craft. He
was able, over a period of more than a year during 2001
and 2002, to hack into nearly 100 military and space
administration sites in pursuit of his quest. Sometimes
he disrupted systems, at one point completely paralyzing
ammunition deliveries to the US Navy's Atlantic Fleet.[53]
In the wake of the investigation that found and fingered
McKinnon, American authorities went after him with
gusto, pursuing an indictment with multiple charges
that could have led to his incarceration for 70 years.

Given concerns over his mental state, and about what he might do to himself if extradited to the United States, a decade-long legal battle unfolded. In the end (October 2012), the United Kingdom's then-Home Secretary, Theresa May, announced the decision to block extradition on the basis of fears that McKinnon might kill himself. And, just a few months later, the decision was taken that he would not be indicted in Britain either.[54] A small mercy; and perhaps a sign of at least some awareness that the hacker is not always to be treated as pariah.

It is ironic that one of the world's most open societies, the United States, should pursue such a harsh legalistic approach to dealing with hackers, while authoritarian Russia embraces, recruits, and often rewards them. During the McKinnon affair, I joined many – including Boris Johnson – who opposed extradition, and will always treasure the thanks I received from McKinnon's mother for speaking out. At the time, I used the analogy of the Nazi rocket scientists, who led the way to outer space, saying it "is as if, after World War II, the Russians were using these rocket scientists while we put the ones we got on trial and incarcerated them."[55] I have often noted how, in that earlier era, the United States was far more pragmatic about the recruitment of those with vital expertise. Wernher von Braun, the Nazi who led the German rocket program in World War II, became a great favorite of the American people – of President Eisenhower, too, who named him head of the Marshall Space Flight Center in July 1960, a position he held for 10 years. I still remember hero-worshipping him, and going to see the film about his life, *I Aim at the Stars*, when I was in grade school back in 1960. The problem we all conveniently overlooked was that, though he may have aimed for the stars, more often than not he hit London.

Today's great master hackers are the latter-day counterparts to those pioneering rocket scientists who led the way to outer space. Nations that neglect or mistreat hackers who can and want to help – those who have the ability to lead the way to security, and hopefully peace, in cyberspace – do so at their increasing peril. They also miss the opportunity to give the very best training to their own military cyber cadres. China and Russia are just two of the leading nations that have clearly embraced the best hackers, and are growing cyberwarriors within their own military services. As does North Korea, a leading recruiter of cyberwarriors among mid-level powers.

Another model, of a kind of cyber militia, has been pioneered by Estonia, whose "Cyber Defense League" volunteers have helped immeasurably to protect their country's critical information infrastructure. For example, the NotPetya cyber attack of 2017, which hit more than 60 countries, inflicting about $10 billion in damage, did not penetrate Estonian cyberspace. Indeed, as one report put it, Estonia "was virtually untouched by this attack."[56] Its cyber militia played a big role in this defensive success. Such militias can contribute significantly to improving a nation's defensive cyber capacities, helping to prevent intrusions, and in rapid response to them. They may also fill the ranks with soldiers able to wage a new kind of war.

3

The Next Face of Battle

All wars are, to one degree or another, time portals through which one can catch glimpses of both past and future. The campaign to overthrow the Taliban and drive al Qaeda from Afghanistan in late 2001 was no exception, combining horse-cavalry operations with the kind of supreme tactical agility enabled by the availability and swift sharing of information that form the core of the military dimension of cyberwar: *Bitskrieg*. Once the decision had been taken to invade Afghanistan in the wake of the 9/11 attacks on America, it was clear that the action would ultimately need to be undertaken by a very small contingent of Green Berets, because mustering and moving a larger force would have taken months, and depended on the willingness of at least one of landlocked Afghanistan's neighbors to allow such an expedition to transit and/or overfly its territory. The Green Berets rode alongside several thousand local tribal allies who had been fighting the Taliban, but who had lost a string of battles to those arch-fundamentalists. Still, with just this handful of

Americans on the ground, supported by attack aircraft above, the once badly beaten "Northern Alliance" now completely reversed its fortunes and saw the Taliban and al Qaeda decisively defeated in just a few weeks of field operations. How did this happen?

The United States Secretary of Defense at the time, Donald Rumsfeld, must receive credit for pushing hard for this "small-footprint," information-enabled campaign. He had to overcome the senior leaders of the uniformed services, who preferred taking a more conventional approach. As journalist Bob Woodward related the high-level wrangling, Rumsfeld "was relentless" in pressing for deployment of the Green Berets. He finally won out over resistance, at which point, as Woodward noted, "Senior generals put their heads down on their desks in despair."[1] They all feared a disaster due to the small numbers of US troops, which would be in harm's way. But they need not have worried so, for the campaign unfolded swiftly, decisively, and at very low cost to the Americans and their Afghan Allies.

It was almost exactly the kind of field campaign that David Ronfeldt and I had envisioned in our 1993 article "Cyberwar Is Coming!" Small, networked teams "swarmed" a much larger enemy whose forces numbered in the range of *80,000* fighters – even more when loosely affiliated tribal allies of the Taliban are counted. Thus was the "Afghan Model" born – an approach that showed how small units on the ground, connected with each other and attack aircraft at the ready above, could strike swiftly, lethally.[2]

For me, the most memorable example of the power of networking the force via the "Tactical Web Page" – a secure intranet link – arose one night in November 2001 when a few special operators struck a devastating blow against the Taliban. "Rick," a spec ops aviator, was flying a night mission toward Kabul from the north when he spotted several flashes below.[3] At first, he thought it was ground fire. But he also knew that the rough road running west from the Taliban stronghold at Mazar-e-Sharif was right under him at that moment, and bouncing vehicles' headlights, even if hooded, might be the source. So he radioed in a report. "Ben," in charge of special operations aircraft, took this information in and had it posted on the Tactical Web Page to the A-team operating in that vicinity. A team member under "Dan's" command – someone in the field *always* kept an eye on the Page – saw the message, woke Dan, and informed him. Dan saw from the given coordinates that he could move quickly to a height from which he could see the road with his long-range night vision equipment. In anticipation, Ben had already ordered up a gunship in case Dan confirmed the sighting. Dan did. When Rick was returning from his mission over Kabul, he looked down at the area in question and saw what he told me was "a ribbon of fire."

That night, over 100 troop-laden Taliban trucks were destroyed. This was *Bitskrieg* in action: the skillful blending of fast-moving information and firepower in swift, lethal fashion. The Taliban truck convoy was destined to be on that road for hours, vulnerable for more than enough time for an aware enemy to strike at it. But the key to that awareness was alert reporting and an information management system that made quick action possible. This incident was hardly the exception in the initial Afghan campaign. Over the next few weeks, *all* of the A-teams used their networking advantage over the enemy, soon toppling the Taliban and driving al Qaeda from Afghanistan.[4]

Beyond this heady success in the field, I was especially pleased by Donald Rumsfeld's having determined to proceed in this way, even in the face of stiff resistance from senior military leaders. This was just the sort of opportunity to conduct war in a new way that he and I had first discussed over lunch at a conference at the RAND Corporation back in 1994. Rumsfeld, greatly pleased with the result, saw Operation Enduring Freedom, as it was called, as heralding a full transformation of the American military – perhaps of warfare itself.[5] He was right, for a while, until old Pentagonian habits of mind reasserted more traditional concepts of operations.

After the initial campaign in late 2001, the same general officers who opposed setting the A-teams loose succeeded in sending over 100,000 troops to Afghanistan, convinced allies to send additional tens of thousands of *their* soldiers, and saw the gains made by the initial *Bitskrieg* approach slowly dissipate before their eyes. This tragedy was avoidable. But even a Secretary of Defense is just a small part of a large organization. Rumsfeld's call for transformation was resisted, and so the war in Afghanistan became much more conventional over the years, with nearly 200,000 Allied troops eventually posted there – as the situation kept deteriorating – until recent drawdowns to levels on a par with the initial campaign were sensibly made. Still, this may have come too late. At present (late 2020), American weariness with the intervention in Afghanistan has led to peace talks that risk handing that tortured land back to the very government we overthrew because it had harbored the terrorists who attacked America on 9/11.

And Afghanistan wasn't alone in becoming a military quagmire. Just two years after the initial success in Afghanistan, Donald Rumsfeld was unable to make the case for a small-footprint invasion of Iraq. Instead, the initial wave was of over 200,000 troops – even more when air force and naval personnel were fully counted.

Conventional Iraqi forces were swiftly defeated; but insurgents created problems for years – and still do.

The Iraqi insurgency led to Rumsfeld's fall at the end of 2006; and his departure as Secretary of Defense greatly energized and re-empowered those traditionalists whose mindsets were far more steeped in the *Blitzkrieg* era than in the potentialities of *Bitskrieg*. To be sure, the notions of cyberspace-based operations that had been bruited about for years remained a part of the strategic discourse; but the emphasis now was largely on how infrastructure could be protected against hackers. As to the military itself, there was interest both in avoiding a "Digital Pearl Harbor" and in crafting capabilities for launching mass-disruptive attacks from cyberspace. But the idea that actual warfighting – in the field, at sea, and in the aerospace environment – could be transformed by the skillful management of informational resources and capabilities withered. This sort of retrogression, hard as it is to experience at first hand, as so many of us who seek a new way forward have done – and which has imposed heavy costs on the soldiers who have served in, and the civilian populations of, Afghanistan and Iraq – is hardly new. As I pointed out in an earlier study of the resistance to change in military affairs, "War is the most dangerous of all human enterprises."[6] Therefore, militaries are reluctant to discard older ways, with generally successful track records, for uncertain new methods. It is worth keeping the past in mind as we ponder the cyber future.

The lengthy paths of military innovation – then and now

Major technological changes have almost always reshaped the ways in which modern wars have been

waged, from the cut-and-thrust of sharp tactical engagements to the overall conduct of whole campaigns.
Rifles, at the Battle of New Orleans in January
1815 – the first with one side armed for the most part
with them – saw a larger British force, deeply experienced from fighting the French in Spain, badly beaten
by unproven, but far more lethally armed, Americans.[7]
The rifle ensured that infantry in battle would ever after
have to engage at greater range, and that the cost of
closing with the enemy would rise steeply. A century
later, the torpedo-armed submarine signaled a revolution
in naval warfare when the German *U-9* and its crew
of a few dozen sank *three* British cruisers in a brief
action in September 1914.[8] The Royal Navy lost 1,500
sailors that day, and soon faced a challenge from these
"raiders of the deep," who nearly starved Britain into
submission. The submarine continued its lethal ways in
World War II, and remains as deadly today. As to attack
aircraft, they too have had transformational effects
on land and naval battles over the past century. The
question now, though, is whether advanced information
technologies will have a similar impact.

The answer to this question will be much facilitated by
recognizing that game-changing technologies that have
profoundly affected the course and conduct of military
affairs do not generally emerge – with the notable
exception of the atomic bomb – like shocking "bolts
from the blue." For example, the rifle that decimated
the Redcoats at New Orleans in 1815 was a weapons
type that had been selected by Louis XIV, in 1679, to
become the standard-issue weapon of French cavalry
companies.[9] The Seven Years' War (1756–63) featured
rifles in some of the fighting, in both Europe and
North America – as did the American Revolution, and
to some extent the Napoleonic Wars as well. But it
took 136 years from Louis XIV's order to his cavalry

squadrons for a battle to be fought by one side heavily armed with rifles. Interestingly, it took *138* years from first use of the submarine in battle – David Bushnell's *Turtle*, which attacked Admiral Howe's flagship at the outset of the American Revolution – to the exploits of the *U-9* and, soon after, of its fellow subs. Aircraft have followed a long path, too, from the French Army's balloonists of 1794 *(compagnie d'aérostiers)* to the biplanes of 1914 – a period of 120 years. Even if one reckons only from the Wright Brothers' first airplane flight in 1903 to the dawn of *Blitzkrieg* in 1939, it still took over a generation for this technology to actualize its lethal potential.

The antecedents of and timeline for the rise of modern, technology-based cyberwar are more complex than the origins and history of the rifle, submarine, and aircraft. This is because of the varied nature and functions of the types of information systems themselves. The earliest of the modern information technologies put to military use was Morse's electric telegraph, which debuted in 1844 and was in wide use on both sides of the Civil War 20 years later, and in the German wars of unification (1866 and 1870–1). In Prussia's victorious conflicts, first against Austria, then France, skillful use of the telegraph played a key role. In the American case, telegraphy enabled a broad "cordon offensive," while in Prussia's wars the telegraph allowed dispersed field armies to coalesce on chosen battle-fields at just the right time. It is important to add, though, that optical telegraphs had been in use since the Byzantines pioneered them a millennium earlier, and worked so well that, as J. B. Bury put it, "a Saracen raid in the Taurus, four hundred miles straight away, could be signaled almost at once to Constantinople."[10] This swift movement of information acted as early warning system and force multiplier for the often-outnumbered

Byzantines. Napoleon, too, employed an optical telegraph, to enhance the effectiveness of his field forces and to administer the affairs of the Empire from wherever he happened to be.

By World War I, half a century after the American Civil War, the telegraph had been joined by radio and telephony. The radio in particular had a profound effect on naval warfare, as the German surface raiders – whose aim was to decimate British and Allied commercial shipping by waging a hard-hitting *guerre de course* – were quickly hunted down because their prey were able, all too often, to send off warnings and their exact positions before they sank. So, in just over four months from the start of the war, as Cyril Falls noted, "Britain had swept virtually all German surface warships off the trade routes."[11] The Allied Signal Detection Investigation Committee (ASDIC) created an early form of sonar during World War I as well, reducing to at least some degree the U-boats' advantage in stealth. But perhaps the most important tech-based coup of World War I was Britain's "hack" of cable traffic, which intercepted and decrypted a message that spoke to the possibility of Mexico joining the German side, with the prospect of regaining some territories previously lost to the United States. Americans were outraged when content of the message was made public; this hacker coup contributed to the American decision to go to war with Germany in 1917.[12]

By the time the Second World War broke out in 1939, information technologies had advanced sharply. Radar ("radio detection and ranging") – conceived in the late 1880s when Heinrich Hertz showed how radio waves could be sent out and would bounce back off metallic objects, then in the early 1900s demonstrated as an aid to navigation in conditions of poor visibility – had by the mid-1930s come into its own. Not only in terms of its revolutionary implications for naval warfare, but with regard to its ability to provide early warning of air attacks on land-based targets. Indeed, Britain's "Chain Home" coastal radars played a crucial role in defeating the German air offensive in the autumn of 1940. And when short-wave radars became small enough to be used in aircraft, this sensing technology's effects on the overall conflict became truly profound. As Robert Morris Page, one of the leading scientists who helped to guide this "sensory revolution," summed up its contributions in the Second World War, "radar . . . won the Battle of Britain, drove the [enemy] submarines from the oceans, and turned [early] Allied defeat into victory."[13] And in all the years since, through the Cold War and on into this "cool war" era, radar has continued to be a vital component of all approaches to battle. On land, at sea, and in the aerospace realm.

World War II also turned out to be a proving ground for computers, especially in terms of the codebreaking hacks engineered by the "boffins" of Bletchley Park, described in the previous chapter. But British Ultra relied upon high-performance computing technology; there were also much more modest computers in use – in combat. For example, the Norden bombsight took charge of the plane, typically the leader of a formation, piloting it over the target, adjusting for wind and other factors. So, in this instance, human pilots of following aircraft would hew rigidly to the guidance of *a machine*. Notoriously over-hyped as being able to "drop a bomb in a pickle barrel from 20,000 feet," the bombsight was in very wide use by a range of types of American bomber aircraft. The *Enola Gay* that dropped an atomic bomb on Hiroshima (arguably needlessly) employed the Norden device as well.

Basic computers were used at sea as well, by both Axis and Allied submariners, to perform ranging and mutual movement calculations essential to hitting their targets. The American Torpedo Data Computer proved to be a very highly effective piece of technology, as it received "data from the periscope and sonar on the enemy's bearing, range, and angle on the bow . . . automatically plotted the course of the enemy relative to the course of the submarine and computed *and set* the proper gyro angle in the torpedo."[14]

This trend toward reliance on computers in battle grew in the decades after World War II, though in Korea and Vietnam their potential was never fully actualized. Massive swarms of Chinese infantry in Korea, and elusive Vietcong irregulars a decade later, posed problems that largely limited the role of computers to assisting in the management of the bombing campaigns conducted during these conflicts. The same was true of efforts to deal with the rise of modern terrorism in the late 1960s, characterized early on by the perils posed by the Irish Republican Army and the Palestinian jihadists. The computer simply seemed to have fewer uses in such irregular conflicts. But the situation started to change in the mid-1970s, as NATO strove to come to terms with its fresh realization that the Russians had a significant advantage in terms of their so-called "conventional forces," which were augmented by a variety of atomic weapons whose deterrent power was likely to keep a war in Europe from escalating to actual nuclear use. In the face of this dilemma, NATO improved its conventional defenses by creating smart weapons – that is, those with sophisticated "information packages" to guide them precisely to their targets – and increasingly complex, computer-enabled command and control systems to coordinate air and ground forces' actions in what came to be known as the AirLand Battle doctrine.[15]

Even as this "precision revolution" was getting under way, though, there were thoughtful voices that, while cognizant of the growing ability to use information systems to powerful effect, saw that the very same advanced technology tools that enhanced NATO's fighting capabilities also *imperiled* them. Should smaller Allied forces, armed with their smart weapons and nimble, networked, command and coordination arrangements, have their guidance systems or communications infrastructures jammed or otherwise disrupted, then the more numerous Warsaw Pact forces could roll west with virtual impunity. Thomas Rona was the visionary who glimpsed both the promise and the danger of building and relying upon a highly "informatized" force, in his seminal 1976 study "Weapon Systems and Information War."[16]

Added to this double-edged notion about the increasing dependence of modern forces on secure, available information systems was a growing sense of skepticism about whether computers – getting ever smaller and more able to be included in tanks, artillery batteries, and a wide range of other weapons – would actually hold up under the rigors of combat. This matter became a subject of heated debate in the 1980s, with each side "having its innings."[17]

First rumblings of cyberwar's specifically military dimension: *Bitskrieg*

The Gulf War of 1990–1 provided the first major opportunity to put the resilience of battlefield computers to a tough test; Iraqi forces were large, well armed, and veterans of an eight-year war with Iran that had only been recently concluded. In addition to the size and complexity of the operations planned, the harsh desert environment was going to put battlefield computers to a rigorous test. This fight looked to be a tough one; but it wasn't, as some of us who worked for General Norman Schwarzkopf, the Allied commander, predicted. The reason: tactical information systems worked reliably, and the creation of the Joint Surveillance and Target Acquisition Radar System (JSTARS), so closely inter-linked to all friendly forces, worked at the broader operational level to give the Allies a full, synoptic view of the battlespace. By comparison, Saddam Hussein's troops had to fight virtually blind. It was this information edge that enabled a lop-sided victory to be won in just over 96 hours of operations on the ground. To many, this desert victory signaled the possibility of a true revolution in military affairs – one largely driven by advances in information technologies.[18] For me, it suggested the possibility of moving beyond the AirLand Battle doctrine, to *Bitskrieg*.

Operation Desert Storm planted the seeds of thought that David Ronfeldt and I nurtured in "Cyberwar Is Coming!" This article, which appeared in the international journal *Comparative Strategy* in 1993, has sparked debates for decades. Yet I remain bemused that the brief discourse on cyberspace operations in our article has received the most attention. For the true focus of our study was to make the case that advanced information technology had profound implications for military organization, doctrine, and strategy. Cyberwar would entail changes in each of these areas: e.g., from larger formations to smaller, nimbler, highly networked units; from mass-on-mass engagements to supple swarm battle tactics; and to the larger strategic goal of "knowing more" than the enemy – about the composition, disposition, and intentions of the forces on both sides.

Sad to say, most militaries have simply grafted on new information technology tools to existing practices, whether for maneuver warfare on land or for aircraft carrier battles at sea, as has been the dominant perspective – and whenever possible the practice – since World War II. That NATO won clumsily in Kosovo in 1999, and that Allied forces have stumbled repeatedly in the wars arising in the wake of 9/11, says quite a bit about the military penchant for adopting new tools while still clinging to older practices.

At this writing (2020), the situation in Afghanistan is still tenuous, and the same goes for Iraq, too. The trillions of dollars spent and thousands of lives lost or shattered in these wars have resulted only in the resurgence of the Taliban in Afghanistan and the rise of a two-front irregular war in Iraq, where both ISIS guerrillas and Iran-backed militias are still posing a vexing strategic challenge. The responsibility for these sad results rests largely upon US military leadership – NATO and other Allies have tended to follow the American lead – whose approach has been traditional, and for the most part conventional, characterized by raids, bombing, and a preference for large-scale firefights whenever possible. But even those charged with formulating strategy in these wars have admitted their lack of openness to trying a fresh approach. As Douglas Lute, who directed Afghan strategy for several years, admitted after stepping down, "We didn't know what we were doing."[19] So he and others did what they knew – rather than strive to gain an information advantage, by various technological and more "human-based" means, then to launch the kind of *Bitskrieg* that was possible in Kosovo, and which was the actual approach used in the opening phase of the war in Afghanistan. The kind of cyberwar David Ronfeldt and I envisioned, and the appropriate doctrine for fighting its battles, can work in conventional *and* irregular wars.

Meet AI Jane

One of the ironies of the current technological era, as it relates to military affairs, is that the age-old effort to use drill and discipline to keep soldiers fighting under the worst conditions – in short, to make them behave like automata in the face of mortal danger[20] – is now being reversed. Advances in artificial intelligence (AI) have quickened their pace so significantly, and the range of automated weapons has opened up so widely, that the perceived challenge now is to reach a point where automata behave more like humans. And, to the extent to which ideas that David Ronfeldt and I have advanced about new battle concepts have caught on, they have gained traction among scientists and operations specialists who believe that robots will become the principal tools for advancing military affairs from *Blitzkrieg* to *Bitskrieg*. For example, our concept of swarming – i.e., simultaneous, omni-directional attack – is seen as a real game-changer when employed by robots. As P. W. Singer has put it, "there is no limit on the size of [robot] swarms . . . iRobot has already run programs with swarms sized up to ten thousand."[21]

This possibility of having intelligent machines do the fighting and make their own decisions about target selection, without a human finger on the trigger (NB: remote-control weapons still have a "human in the loop") marks a true inflection point in strategic thought. Manuel De Landa put the matter starkly when he noted, "the moment autonomous weapons begin to select their own targets, the moment the responsibility of establishing whether a human is friend or foe is given to the machine, we will have crossed a threshold and a new era will have begun."[22] True enough, but it does beg the question of exactly how the machines will be programmed to fight. For visionaries such as Peter Singer, the answer is clearly to employ radically new battle doctrines like swarming. But what if the warbots are programmed to fight with older concepts of operations in mind? A sample of old-style thinking can be found in John Ringo and Travis Taylor's novel of a conflict waged between robots and humans, *Von Neumann's War*.[23] The machines, though swift, powerful, and to some extent adaptive, still have a fundamentally conventional "mindset" to their programming – so the humans defeat them. The point here is that, just because a smart robot is doing the fighting, that doesn't make it *Bitskrieg*. Programming is all.

And, beyond the matter of how to program robots, the issue of the future landscape of conflict should not be seen in terms either of complete replacement of human presence in battle or of just the incremental addition of robots in select situations. The key to cyberwar, and its associated *Bitskrieg* battle doctrine, is in attaining an information advantage – that is, to have and use more information, or to make swifter use of the level of information to which both sides in a war might have equal access. The edge in *awareness* is the heart of cyberwar. Undeniably, robots can do more of the fighting in place of humans in the future. As far back as 1996, James Dunnigan was envisioning bots in land battles, fighting in the most exposed forward spots, so that they would "take the heat instead of humans." But he still saw flesh-and-blood soldiers in the field as well. Similarly, he envisioned ships whose crews were increasingly robotized, but with small human complements as well. The same, he felt, would be true of air power, with some planes in a squadron piloted autonomously by robots, others perhaps remote-controlled, and some with human pilots. As Dunnigan perceived the situation, "piloted and pilotless aircraft will coexist."[24]

Yes, robots will form an important part of the *Bitskrieg* era; but "bots in battle," alone, will not likely suffice.

Information will. Lots of it, usable to gain a clearer picture of the enemy's positions, movements, and intentions – on land, at sea, and in the aerospace environment. In this function, the gaining and sustaining of an information edge, robots may play a most important role in the future of conflict. Not only in terms of processing, sorting, and structuring massive data flows produced by intelligence, surveillance, and reconnaissance (ISR) systems – some already automated – but in ensuring that vital information is made swiftly available to forces operating at the leading edge of the battle. Instead of centralized, hierarchical "command and control," a networked approach that shares data widely will create a situation where, in the view of RAND analysts Brian Nichiporuk and Carl Builder, "smaller units may operate more freely and autonomously."[25] This is the watershed insight into how information systems, when their potential can be fully actualized, will enable an entirely new approach to military affairs. Manuel De Landa was aware of this point, too, when he said (quite early, back in 1991): "Today's computerized networks, for instance, are imposing on the military the need to decentralize control schemes, just as the conoidal bullet forced it in the nineteenth century to decentralize its tactical schemes."[26]

The insight here is that technological advances in information systems may imply a need to redesign organizational structures. But this insight has just as clearly not yet imposed on militaries an understanding of the need to shift from a hierarchical to a networked perspective regarding information flows and organizational forms. Most advanced militaries are still intent upon centralizing communications and retaining their large unit structures – divisions and brigades on land, fleets and task forces at sea, and groups and wings in the air – which have dominated military affairs over the past century and more. The adherence of militaries to their "few-large" organizational structures is a vestige of industrial-age thinking. In the mass production era, the greater the concentration of force, the stronger its effect in battle. But in an Information Age replete with ever smarter, long-ranging, often automated weapons, it will be far better to distribute forces widely – humans and bots. And the best way to organize will be to shift to a "many-small" paradigm. By increasing the number of units of action – of much reduced size – they can be well dispersed, so as to reduce their vulnerability to being targeted, but will still be able to coordinate their fire, from many directions, on a traditionally massed enemy force. A networked organizational redesign allows for the kind of swarm tactics that Ronfeldt and I have advocated.[27]

There has been increasing support for the swarming concept since we introduced it, particularly in naval affairs. Indeed, three key United States Navy admirals each brought fresh perspectives to the swarming concept that fully recognized the importance of human–machine teaming. The first was Arthur Cebrowski, with his concept of network-centric warfare. He was followed by Thomas Rowden, who developed the doctrine of "distributed lethality." Most recently, during his time as Chief of Naval Operations, John Richardson introduced the broadest concept of all: the "networked Navy," in which information flows are to be swift and widespread, enabling far more ships, planes, submarines – as well as fully automated systems – to fight in decentralized unison.[28] Despite such affirmations from visionaries in high command, Ronfeldt and I have, from time to time, still had to remind the broader military audience that networking and swarming are not the sole province of robots.[29] The most significant gains in military effectiveness are going to come from skillful blending of humans and intelligent machines in the kinds of combat formations that Dunnigan envisioned, which can employ battle doctrines such as swarming, *together.*

This vision of the next face of battle as featuring dispersion of units of action that are nevertheless capable of coordination and of highly innovative tactics has a vulnerability: its dependence on very secure, readily available communications, both with other fighting formations and with higher-level commands. Given the complexity and likely high tempo of operations, AI will play a key role. Not just as part of the order of battle, but in helping to keep communications open and sensors functioning. Enemy leaders will quickly realize that disruption – or, better, exploitation – of the information systems that tie together a dispersed opposing force can make its individual components vulnerable to defeat in detail. This is much as Allied codebreakers hacked the German Enigma system during World War II, helping to locate and destroy the widely distributed U-boats that had previously, with relative impunity, swarmed convoys in attacking "wolf packs" that were guided to their targets by coded radio messages.[30] An additional vulnerability of any force that includes or relies upon robots is their susceptibility to varied forms of electro-magnetic pulse (EMP) weapons, ranging from very high-altitude – above 25 miles up – nuclear bursts to smaller-scale, directed energy systems. Experts see this vulnerability as particularly grave.[31]

Thus, the paradox of AI Jane's rise is that, for all the gains robots bring to processes of "sensing and shooting," they are in some ways more vulnerable than humans, given that just disrupting them is as valuable as destroying them. They can be disrupted by being hacked, hit with ordnance, or by their circuits being fried by electromagnetic means. That said, humans will prove targetable electronically, too, if the trend toward using smart implants – currently focused on dealing with bacterial and sleep pattern problems – continues. Indeed, a study of the "Havana Syndrome" has concluded that American personnel in Cuba, and CIA operatives elsewhere, have already been subjected to attack by directed-energy weapons.[32]

In a looming era in which AI and other advances in the information technology sphere will newly empower armed forces, the ability to target their vulnerabilities in multiple ways truly holds at risk the vision of an "automated battlefield" that has captivated senior leaders of many of the world's most modern militaries for over half a century. General William Westmoreland – who oversaw for years the American quagmire in Vietnam, then went on to become the Army Chief of Staff – was an articulate advocate for automation. As he put the matter in a speech to the Association of the US Army in October 1969:

> On the battlefield of the future enemy forces will be located, tracked and targeted almost instantaneously through the use of data-links, computer-assisted intelligence evaluation and automated fire control. With first-round kill probabilities approaching certainty, and with surveillance devices that can continuously track the enemy, the need for large forces to fix the opposition physically will be less important . . . I see battlefields that are under 24-hour real- or near-real-time surveillance of all types. I see battlefields on which we can destroy anything we locate through instant communications and almost instantaneous application of highly lethal firepower.[33]

Westmoreland glimpsed the key factors: the information edge; the downsizing of forces; and the extreme accuracy of weapons systems. The components of *Bitskrieg*. Still, one has to anticipate that thinking enemies will prepare ways to hold such systems at risk of being disrupted, destroyed, or deceived. How to mitigate this risk? In terms of secure communications, moving from the current reliance on a relatively small number of sizable satellites to large numbers of tiny "cube sats" is the answer – highlighting again the benefit of shifting from few-large to many-small. The value of networked cube sats lies in the wider, more time-persistent coverage they can provide in a theatre of operations. By sharing their data, a far more comprehensive picture of the action can be derived. Also, the small size and cost of a cube will make it easier to replace network nodes if individual sats are shot down or blinded. As to terrestrial operations, improved information security requires shifting from Maginot-Line-like reliance on firewalls and anti-virals – so easy to outflank or penetrate – to embracing the ubiquitous use of strong encryption and Cloud computing instead. The bots themselves will have to be built with strong shielding against electronic attack. Human soldiers have body armor; automata will need to have good "bot armor."

The intelligent machine as strategist?

Thus far, I have focused for the most part on tactical matters that will bear upon the diffusion of automated, increasingly intelligent systems on the battlespaces of the future. But there is also a way to think about AI having an opportunity to enhance operations at the strategic level, too. An idea that I have been developing with the US Defense Advanced Research Projects Agency (DARPA), for example, is focused on the use of automation as an adjunct to human strategic planning processes. The basic concept is that strategic factors are generally known – even if details sometimes elude our ability to calculate with high reliability – and that machine learning, a key aspect of AI along with its suppleness in the handling of "big data," may provide fresh insights for planners and decision makers to ponder. The name I have given to my concept is a "comprehensive, automated strategy evaluation engine" (CASEE, pronounced "Casey"). For now, due to the sensitivity of the undertaking, I have to be sketchy about specifics. But the basic point is that, if one really believes machines can "learn," and that true "intelligence" can be silicon- rather than just carbon-based, then it is high time to include AI in the process of strategy-making.

To date, AIs have proved sufficiently good strategists to beat the world champions of chess, poker, and *weiqi*. There is even some evidence that AI can hold its own in top-tier forensics, in the form of IBM's Project Debater. This AI, developed at an IBM lab in Israel over the past decade, held its own in complex argument – first, over subsidization of space exploration, then as to the value of telemedicine – with national-champion debaters at an event in San Francisco in 2018. As judged by the audience, the AI lost once and won once. This should be seen as an important inflection point in the course of AI development, as reasoned argument over many-sided issues is clearly a hallmark of strategic thinking. As one incisive report of the event described it, "the Debater's" success reflected AI's growing ability to assist decision-making processes because it is able to "take all the evidence and arguments into account and challenge the reasoning of humans when necessary."[34] It seems clear to me that the Project Debater team ought now to have a go at military affairs as well.

Given all the costly difficulties with the American-led post-9/11 wars in Afghanistan and Iraq – as well as with the problematic limited interventions in Libya, Somalia, and Syria – there is surely need for a fresh approach. AI can clear away some of the cobwebs, bringing clarity.

Without doubt, modern warfare is more complex than chess, poker, or *weiqi* – debate, too. For, aside from purely military matters, there are many political, social, and economic factors that will come into play at the strategic level. But even these can be modeled, if in abstracted fashion. I know from experience. During the most difficult period of the Iraqi insurgency that arose in the wake of the invasion of that country in 2003 – led largely by Anglo-American forces – I developed a handwritten version of CASEE. I was inspired by the example of Alan Turing, who employed pen and paper to write the first chess-playing computer program with his colleague David Champernowne in 1948. Two years later, he simulated the computer, strictly adhering to his simple "search and point-count" paper program in a game against his colleague Alick Glennie. The program lost in 29 moves.[35] In my case, though, I had a bit better luck with my hand-written program: CASEE came up with the organizational idea of shifting coalition forces from being mostly positioned on huge FOBs to redeploying them to a range of very small, platoon-sized outposts. CASEE also urged reaching out directly to insurgents, offering them the opportunity to switch sides against the "foreign fighters" who were exploiting Iraqi patriots for their own dark purposes.

The CASEE-generated concept of "outpost and outreach" eventually found a following – among like-minded officers, at both junior and senior levels, some of whom had begun to think along these lines on their own.

It was adopted in late 2006 and early 2007, and swiftly led to a 90 percent drop in Iraqi civilian casualties that persisted for years. Not bad for a rudimentary program. It did something AI can do very well: take a complex, "wicked" problem and break it into digestible chunks. In this case, the focus was on the manner in which coalition forces were deployed, and on the possibility that there was a divide in motivation between Iraqis and al Qaeda foreign fighters who, according to much of the evidence available, were increasingly using the former as cannon fodder for their own purposes. The point is that CASEE didn't have to solve *everything* about Iraq; just two operational changes – creating small outposts, and engaging in systematic outreach to indigenous insurgents – had the potential to change the dynamics of the fighting on the ground.[36] The results of these changes were swiftly felt and dramatic – their impact mattering more than the contemporaneous addition of a small number of "surge troops."[37]

If primitive CASEE could do this, clearly there is much promise for AI in the realm of strategic planning, not just battle tactics. And, just as Turing began development of strategic artificial intelligence with his pen-and-paper program over 70 years ago, the next steps in true, high-level machine learning will likely begin with non-technological conceptualizing. A good term for this method is Peter Denning's "computational thinking."[38] I must also note that my design for CASEE owes much to an earlier pen-and-paper "program" that Paul Davis and I developed at RAND back in 1990, when we were asked to help senior military leaders to think about the crisis with Saddam Hussein. Adhering to our programming constraints, we were nevertheless able to predict that Saddam would not push on from Kuwait into Saudi Arabia, and that bombing alone would not dislodge him.[39]

So, when we think of AI Jane in the future, perhaps we should be open as to the *rank* she might hold. For if an intelligent machine can strategize with the best of the humans, then AI is truly capable of generalship.

But for now, the emphasis is tactical, and in the future. Some version of AI Jane will serve alongside infantry in battle, in squadrons with human "buddies" in aerial dogfights, and with sailors on ships and submarines in naval actions. To some extent, this human–machine teaming is already going on, and it is fascinating to see how often soldiers have bonded with their AI comrades – even to the point of mourning their "deaths" in formal burial ceremonies when they are lost in battle.[40] One particularly successful PackBot, "Scooby Doo" – bots are also known to be named, sometimes, for their soldier-partners' wives – that had saved many lives by dealing with deadly impro-vised explosive devices in Iraq and Afghanistan, was mourned, decorated with a medal, and its shattered remains are now on display at the iRobot museum in Bedford, Massachusetts. Flesh-and-blood soldiers have truly bonded with their AI comrades, as Julie Carpenter, one of the leading scholars of human–machine inter-action, has found.[41] It seems that this new technology is in the process of creating a new sociology, too. At least at the tactical level in military settings – but beyond them, too, in the social domain, potentially in the form of emotionally bonded relationships.[42]

Alluring prospects, fresh concerns

Clearly, advances in information technology have the potential to create the next face of battle. From old-style clashes of massed forces to new swarms of widely distributed small units, armed conflict is soon going to look very different from the vision of fighting for which most advanced militaries – including those of the NATO countries, Russia, China, and others – have prepared. The term of art for this kind of change is a "revolution in military affairs," a concept first fully exposited in the 1950s in a series of Oxford lectures by the historian Michael Roberts. In his scholarship, Roberts noted that transformations are not simply technological; to be truly revolutionary, new tools must engender new practices, in terms of their impact on military organization and doctrine, the complexity of operations, and their overall impact on society. For him, a prime example was provided by refinements to the musket in the mid-1500s, accompanied by fresh doctrinal insight into the value of massed volley fire, rather than firing at will. This practice led to larger-sized fixed formations (battalions, divisions), bigger armies, and much more complex logistics and maneuvers – all of which led to wars being waged on a greater scale that had devastating new impacts on societies.[43]

And when industrialization came along, the ability to produce massive amounts of munitions, and new weapons with which to deliver them – from machine guns to high-explosive artillery, for example – led to further growth in the size of armed forces, now often crammed into the same small physical spaces in which earlier forms of war were waged. Herein lie the origins of the World War I disasters on the clogged-up Western Front and at Gallipoli. For, even in the face of new destructive capacity, senior leaders on all sides tended to use the latest tools in tandem with their centuries-old mantra of massing. This led to untold slaughters, and the ultimate failure of "men against fire," as Sir Michael Howard put the matter in a famous lecture.[44]

The story of the Second World War was less of stalemate, thanks to the rise of mechanization, the increased range and payload-carrying capacity of aircraft, and advances in radio, radar, and code-breaking computers. But, even with the additional impetus that came from fresh, innovative doctrines – *Blitzkrieg* on land, aircraft carrier and submarine swarming tactics at sea, and "strategic" aerial bombing – the various campaigns all devolved, once new tools and practices diffused, into attritional patterns aimed at wearing down the adversary. A pattern that held in Korea and Vietnam as well.

It is a pattern that continued until the information-enabled victory of the Allied coalition over Saddam Hussein in 1991. This was the first hint of the possible emergence of *Bitskrieg,* the military aspect of cyberwar – that is, "cyber's" use for battle, rather than for infrastructure disruption, political agitation, or other sorts of hacks – that drives operations by generating an exploitable information edge over one's opponent. But Operation Desert Storm didn't turn out to be *the* inflection point that led to a revolution in military affairs, as the world's advanced militaries have, for the most part, remained prisoners of their own habits of mind and institutional interests.

New technological tools have come along steadily for the past 30 years and more; too often they have been grafted on to existing practices. Michael Roberts's conditions for revolutionary change – to organizations, doctrines, overall complexity, and societal impact – have not been met. Still, the emergence of cyberwar, and its related military doctrine of *Bitskrieg*, do hold out the prospect of introducing quantum changes into the conduct of warfare: from old-style massed frontal or flank attacks to omnidirectional swarms, from balky divisions and battalions to nimble, networked units of action at the platoon and even squad levels. In strategic terms, there is even the possibility of waging short, sharp wars at lower cost in battle casualties, along with a much-reduced impact on society – a most welcome prospect.

In the United States, Donald Rumsfeld grasped this point and, just six months after the small teams of Green Berets drove the Taliban from power – conducting operations like the one described at the start of this chapter – he issued a powerful statement of the need for change:

> We must begin shifting the balance in our arsenal between manned and unmanned capabilities, between short- and long-range systems, between stealthy and non-stealthy systems, between sensors and shooters, and between vulnerable and hardened systems . . . [We must] communicate and operate seamlessly on the battlefield.[45]

A shift of this sort can enable significant reductions in defense spending, for both advanced and lesser-developed nations. Aside from the fiscal windfall that would accompany adoption of a *Bitskrieg* approach, there would also be the practical benefit that big-ticket, Industrial-Age weapons systems would no longer be lumbering about battlespaces where they are held at increasing risk by a range of deadly new weapons. Given the ever-decreasing ability of Industrial-Age systems – from main battle tanks to super aircraft carriers – to survive in future conflicts replete with smart, often automated, swarms and multitudes of small units armed with hypersonic missiles and other weapons, guided by sophisticated "information packages," this is a good thing. The key insight is that military power will no longer emanate from "platforms," like those super-sized aircraft carriers.

Instead, the emphasis will be on countless small units of action and maneuver, empowered by the increased information content of their weapons and the inter-connectedness of all forces in the field, at sea, and in the aerospace environment. Advances in both sensing and guidance of weapons mean that the tight, ages-old link between distance and accuracy – historically, the farther away a target was, the less likely it would be hit – has been decoupled. As Colin McInnes put the matter so succinctly back in 1992, "accuracy is no longer a function of range."[46] Now, many weapons can have (and some already do have) vastly increased range with extremely high degrees of accuracy.

On top of this, smooth networking allows for far more of the force to be well informed and able to engage the enemy more of the time. Of course, effective networking is wholly dependent upon secure infor-mation systems – a fundamental challenge that must be mastered for real progress in military affairs to take hold. This goal, of having truly secure information systems, remains tantalizingly within reach, but just beyond most militaries' grasp. Yet, with AI Jane helping to form human–machine teams, the prospects will improve for the rise of a *Bitskrieg* doctrine that can have just as much impact on the conduct and course of wars as *Blitzkrieg* doctrine did a century ago.

Will a march to sunny new uplands in military affairs go smoothly? Hardly. Progress will be uneven. Few in the 1920s and 1930s figured out the combat potential of networking tanks and planes by radio, and the attendant organizational and doctrinal implications. Few today appreciate the prospects for transforma-tional change wrought by bits and bytes. A century ago, the Germans led when it came to adopting armored maneuver warfare – *Blitzkrieg* – and the Japanese were marginally ahead of the US Navy in appreciating the manner in which aircraft carriers would soon be changing sea battles. Today, it seems that the Russians, with their small formations of "little green men" and their emerging "Gerasimov Doctrine" that combines cyber and psychological elements with more purely military operations, have the lead in understanding how wars will be fought. The Chinese, too, have keen insight into how information technologies have enabled transformational change, via their notion of "unrestricted warfare."[47]

Interestingly, ideas that Ronfeldt and I advanced in our 1997 study, *In Athena's Camp*, appeared verbatim in People's Liberation Army (PLA) doctrinal documents well before the officially authorized translation was published. And, today, much of the PLA discourse on military affairs is redolent of our concepts. Conversely, few of our recommendations have thrived in the West – and, even in these instances, only in part, embracing: (1) a thin technical slice of our concept of cyberwar; (2) an emphasis on swarming, but only as practiced by automata; and (3) our mantra "It takes a network to fight a network."[48]

Habits of mind and institutional interests will surely condition the global race for advantage in preparing for war in the twenty-first century. Some will speed ahead; laggards, for all their negligence, may yet catch up via inevitable diffusion of technologies and ideas. But, as the historical record suggests, this may only happen after "early adopters" inflict painful lessons during some initial period of conflict, much as Germany and Japan did while landing punishing blows on the Allies in the first three years (1939–42) of World War II. Back then, militaries of the principal Axis Powers presented their leaders with the prospect of achieving swift victories enabled by the very latest technological advances – a vision too tempting to resist.

This is what may be occurring yet again today, as cyberwarfare techniques – from tactical battlefields to the strategic realm of infrastructure disruptions – may make war seem an eminently "thinkable" policy option for potential aggressors. In particular, what seems to be a clear advantage to the side taking the offensive creates instability in crisis, as each side has a strong incentive to strike first. Prior to World War I, railroad transport was the technology that seemed to give a big edge to the side that mobilized and advanced first, greatly contributing to the diplomatic crisis of July 1914 turning into the catastrophic war that erupted with the "guns of August," as Barbara Tuchman noted in her classic study of this tragedy.[49]

In addition to crisis instability – and the consequent undermining of deterrence – that comes with a perceived "first strike" advantage, cyberwar has the added attraction of providing prospects for engaging in what leading Chinese strategists call "remote warfare." This term suggests the possibility of waging war without putting human soldiers, sailors, and airmen at great risk. Michael Pillsbury thoughtfully expanded on the meaning of this Chinese concept, labeling it "remote grappling," so that the spectrum of conflicts and malign actions well short of high-intensity war (e.g., like the massive theft of intellectual property that the Chinese already engage in) is included.[50] When one adds to the "remoteness" of fighting by bits and bytes the increasing presence of armed robots capable of carrying an increasing burden of the responsibility in future battles – the rise of remote-piloted drones merely foreshadows the greater possibilities that would come from full automation – constraints upon and caution about the use of force become ever more attenuated. Looking at the carnage of battle during the US Civil War, Confederate General Robert E. Lee said, "It is well that war is so terrible. Otherwise we should grow too fond of it." Cyberwar seems cleaner and "cooler." There is a risk of quickly growing too fond of it.

The emergence of "fighting robots" may have a range of deleterious effects beyond making *going* to war more likely. In relentless pursuit of their missions, robots may, as Erik Gartzke has noted, prove more likely to inflict greater degrees of damage on civilian infrastructural targets – as well as on innocent noncombatants themselves.[51] Thus, both the classical notions of initiating or entering a war justly (*jus ad bellum*), as well as conducting operations ethically (*jus in bello*) will come under serious pressure, given the attractiveness of the option of employing automata as principal warfighters. This problem can be mitigated by the careful pairing of human soldiers with intelligent machines. But there will still be difficulties. In an urban battle, for example, a robot will likely be sent into a building, instead of a human soldier, with the mission of clearing it. Will the robot distinguish between an enemy soldier and a civilian? Or how about in a more general firefight in the field? Will the robot know when an enemy is wounded? Surrendering? Or just pretending to give up peacefully? A further complication arises with strategic cyber attack, the targets of which will often be civilian systems. Given the fast-paced nature of cyberspace-based operations, automation will play a huge role in such "virtual offensives," making it harder for humans to stop an operation if or when robots overstep rules of engagement – or even to know, in real time, that a violation is occurring. Simply put, cyberwar and *Bitskrieg* pose serious challenges to ethical war-waging. The classical theories of Augustine, Aquinas, and those of Grotius and other moderns, will come under great pressure. Their ideas, based largely on going to war as a last resort and maintaining the immunity of noncombatants,[52] set constraints that appear to run quite contrary to what the new technologies allow.

But the challenges, with automata possibly violating ethical rules of engagement in ambiguous situations, can be mitigated via programming – even in the most difficult combat situations on land. And it should be noted that human soldiers have long had, and still have, problems avoiding the inadvertent killing of the innocent. Sometimes, too, fatigue, anger, or even a cold-blooded desire for revenge can cause humans deliberately to commit atrocities. AI Jane doesn't tire, get mad, or seek payback. Also, in air and naval battles, the bots of war will have a much clearer ability to distinguish friend from foe, making their use in these settings easier to contemplate and more effective – with far less worry about violations of the laws of war. Yet there is more to the ethical issues raised by *Bitskrieg* and other modes of cyberwar than the behavior of bots. For the very possibility of waging short, sharp wars in which a significant information advantage keeps costs and risks low might induce aggressors, or even just those who feel gravely threatened, to resort to the use of force. Worse, the prospect of being able to launch and win wars swiftly may encourage taking so-called "preventive action" – as the American-led coalition claimed it was doing when invading Iraq in 2003 on the basis of the (false) assertion that Saddam Hussein was building a nuclear arsenal. Instead of a walkover, the Allies had a long slog.

Where troubled American and Allied military experiences in post-9/11 conflicts have led thoughtful military leaders to question what General Rupert Smith calls the "utility of force,"[53] cyberwar and its *Bitskrieg* battle application may restore a sense that fighting still has utility. Such a turn of mind is dangerous. It will spark arms racing, weaken deterrence, and, when wars erupt, will encourage escalation. For the country that is falling victim to a blazing-fast *Bitskrieg* may try to retrieve its fortunes by "going nuclear."

Escalation was the long-time strategy of NATO during the decades when the alliance feared being overrun by Warsaw Pact forces. The NATO doctrine of "flexible response" was all about resorting to nuclear weapons if conventional defenses failed. As former US Army Chief of Staff General Maxwell Taylor noted, this doctrine entailed having "a capability to react across the entire spectrum of possible challenge."[54] To make sure that the Russians got the point, every NATO "Reforger" field exercise concluded with a call for nuclear strikes. But today, and tomorrow, perhaps Russia – or North Korea – might threaten nuclear escalation if faced with a seemingly unstoppable *Bitskrieg*. A turnabout twist to flexible response.

Perhaps, just perhaps, the enduring threat of nuclear "mutual assured destruction" will keep even limited use of such weapons in abeyance – but this will depend upon the stakes for which the war is being fought. And it should be noted that, early in the Trump Administration, American strategic posture shifted to a willingness to contemplate the use of nuclear weapons in response to conventional – and even cyber – acts of aggression, if the damage done by the attacker were to reach a serious level. This was a troubling "relaxation of constraints," as one analyst put it, that is likely to embolden other possessors of nuclear weapons.[55] Thus, whatever optimism one might have about the prospects for waging short, sharp wars using the *Bitskrieg* doctrine should be much tempered by an awareness of, and preparation for, the escalatory potential in such situations.

One implication of this concern would be to reinvigorate nuclear arms control. This is a worthy notion. But there may be another way to get at the problem of technological advances making wars easier to contemplate – and more likely to escalate: apply the arms control paradigm to the cyber realm. Success in such an undertaking might lessen the likelihood of wars breaking out in the first place, thus reducing the risks of escalation. Just what "cyber arms control" might look like is explored in the next chapter.

4

(Arms) Ctrl+Alt+Esc

Few statesmen, of any nation, have served in as many diverse ways as Leon Panetta. In the wake of eight terms as a member of the United States House of Representatives, he subsequently served as the Director of the Office of Management and Budget, then as President Bill Clinton's chief of staff. Under Barack Obama, he was first the Director of Central Intelligence, then Secretary of Defense. And, after a long career in public office, he shifted to become a leading "public intellectual," informing and guiding the discourse on a wide range of policy issues, foreign and domestic – a role in which he continues to serve, including as an educator via the Panetta Institute.[1]

Among the matters that he has considered to be of greatest urgency, cybersecurity has been, from early on, very close to the top. Both in the high councils of state and in the broader open media, he has repeatedly warned of a possible "Cyber Pearl Harbor" that could cripple the United States – or *any* country that relies on the steady, sound functioning of an advanced information infrastructure. In this sense, the more traditional security concern about the mass destruction nuclear weapons might cause is now joined by a cyber threat of costly, painful, "mass disruption."

Aside from calling for improved approaches to defending against disruptive hacks, Leon Panetta has also played a leading role in calling for international agreements, by whose terms countries would covenant to refrain from engaging in such attacks. As he put the matter in a speech to the Business Executives for National Security in 2012, diplomacy could be added to defenses in approaching the cybersecurity problem, the goal being to "forge international consensus on the roles and responsibilities of nations to help secure cyber-space."[2] In the wake of these remarks, some experts in the cyber field have called for a serious debate about cyber arms control. James Lewis, an influential scholar of cyber-related affairs, has argued that the only path to true cybersecurity will be via arms control.[3] More recently, Martin Giles has added an ethical/humani-tarian twist to buttress the concept by placing special emphasis on the need to refrain from hacking hospitals and civilian infrastructures.[4] The Wilson Center and the US Army War College have also weighed in on the subject.[5] The discourse is thoughtful.

To be sure, valid concerns have been raised about the difficulties entailed in verifying the size of, and range of weaponry in, cyber "arsenals." As Dorothy Denning noted in a seminal early paper on this challenge, cyber weapons "can be manufactured without any special physical materials or laboratory facilities." She went on to say that such devices could be "easily copied and distributed."[6] Assessment and verification issues have also been considered in a perceptive commentary by the Council on Foreign Relations.[7] Clearly, the matter of monitoring poses a serious challenge.

The flip side of obstacles to oversight is cheating – that is, hiding, denying, or otherwise disguising one's capabilities and resources. While this sort of behavior is a worry in the nuclear realm, it is harder to hide inter-continental ballistic missiles and submarines than it is to conceal computer worms, viruses, and hacker networks. And cyber attacks may be conducted more covertly. Even so, as Harvard's Joseph Nye has asked – and answered – about cyber arms control agreements: "What is to prevent cheating? The answer is self-restraint."[8] I would add "self-interest" in avoiding retaliation.

In addition to monitoring-related issues, two other important concerns have been repeatedly raised. The first has to do with the potential difficulty in gaining the compliance of non-state actors to any agreement reached only by nation-states. Terrorist, transnational criminal (including hacker) and insurgent networks, for example, might reject outright the idea of becoming constrained by a nation-based norm of cyber behavior. And the very idea of including them in formal negotiation for such a treaty is extremely unlikely. Yet this limitation should hardly be seen as sufficiently serious to thwart cyber arms control efforts. Non-state actors are not signatories to behavior-based chemical and biological weapons conventions currently in force, but the participation of the overwhelming majority of nation-states in them has kept the world largely free of both these types of pernicious weapons. In an era suffused with COVID-19, though, the vigilance of nation-states will have to increase, as "barriers to entry" for terrorists seeking biological weapons may fall sharply. Now, instead of the requirement for first-rate scientific skills and secure laboratory facilities, a terrorist organization might simply think in terms of forming cadres of COVID-19 "super spreaders," then sending them out to public squares, transit terminals, malls, and the like.

This is another form of "mass disruption" nations will have to deal with – but which, in comparison, makes monitoring non-state hacker networks seem far less daunting.

The second major concern has to do with whether intelligence gathering is still allowable when conducted via cyberspace means. Nations have always spied on each other; doing so by way of hacking is, in a real sense, just another emerging form of "national technical means," to use the term of art in the espionage business. It is a mode of collection that has the potential to prove superior to spy satellites and other types of viewing or listening devices, given the immediacy and detail that can be derived from a most skillful hack that, say, enables the reconstruction of every keystroke a particular target is making. Or that allows for the illumination of an entire network by means of revealing all its links and nodes via analysis of cyber "traffic." Cyber technical collection capabilities can be described, as I have put the matter – in the Pentagon and elsewhere – as having such high quality that they should be considered a form of "virtual human intelligence." But they are even better, because human agents often suffer from perceptual or motivated biases, or have secret agendas of their own – like "Curveball," the source who told lies about Saddam Hussein having a nuclear program, lies that led to the unjustified invasion of Iraq in 2003.[9] Cyber intelligence – much of which can be gathered by robotic "spiders" searching about in adversary systems – would sharply reduce, if not eliminate, such bias in collection and analysis.

The problem with "virtual human intelligence," alternately known as "clandestine technical collection" in some places, lies in the means by which access is gained to such valuable perches for spying. For it turns out that the very same exploits required to spy on a targeted system can also serve to prepare for extensive acts of "cybotage." The system penetrated for spying purposes is at the same time vulnerable to being seeded with all sorts of the most malicious software, designed to cripple communications and disrupt a nation's critical infrastructures from the very outset of, or during, a war.

The observational equivalence between cyber spying and preparations for cyberwar poses a vexing challenge for any behavior-based arms control regime that might be established. That said, it is a challenge worth taking up, given that in the absence of formal agreement the current situation *is* one in which cyber spying is going on, and may already be accompanied by all sorts of preparations for acts of widely disruptive cybotage. By reaching an agreement that tolerates spying but forbids covert preparation for mounting cyber attacks – among other prohibited activities, such as the theft of intellectual property – nations raise the stakes for each other in ways that may deter acts of cybotage. For example, discovery of a cyber weapon designed to cripple military communications in wartime could lead to abrogation of the treaty and the onset of costly cyber depredations that neither side might want.

During his time in office, President Barack Obama was made fully aware of the growing threats – both to the United States and to the broader world – emanating from cyberspace. Early on, he strove, unsuccessfully, to come to some sort of cyber terms with Moscow. He also understood that China was growing not only as an economic and military power, but as a cyber one as well. With this in mind, he engaged with President Xi Jinping; and during the latter's September 2015 official visit to the United States, the possibility of reaching agreement on behavior-based controls on cyber acts of aggression was discussed. The outline of an accord stated that: (1) neither country would engage in cyber theft of intellectual property; and (2) there would be a ban on state, or state-sponsored, cyber attacks on infrastructures in peacetime.[10] In the years since, the American government has formally charged state, and state-sponsored, Chinese actors with massive cyberspace-based thefts of intellectual property, and even closed Beijing's consulate in Houston. As to the agreement not to attack each other's infrastructures, the qualifier "in peacetime" puts the whole concept into question. What if one nation or the other decides to *start* a war with an infrastructure attack? Since it is at the beginning of a conflict, the "peacetime" limit no longer applies – unless the agreement reached is explicit about *not* opening a war this way.

Whatever the intrinsic merits of cyber arms control may be, it is clear that efforts to pursue such a diplomatic approach have made little practical progress. No doubt this is due to the perceived benefits to be gleaned from hacking others' systems, given the many advances in intrusive cyber tools that have, to date, outstripped the defensive measures taken against them by far, as the December 2020 deep intrusion into several departments of the American government, including the Pentagon, demonstrated.[11] This situation gives piquancy to the point that, a quarter-century ago, there was an outstanding opportunity to avoid a cyber arms race – responsibility for the failure to seize this chance rests largely on the shoulders of American senior leadership.

The missed opportunity

The decade of the 1990s was a time of great ferment in emerging debates about cyberwar. The discourse revolved around issues regarding how broadly or narrowly to define the concept, as well as about the extent to which classic concepts such as arms racing, deterrence, and coercive diplomacy might still prove applicable as guides to statecraft. For Americans, and in some few places across the NATO community, the very idea of cyber arms control seemed unattractive because, as I was often told, "We're ahead."

In terms of the breadth of the cyberwar concept as David Ronfeldt and I developed it, the rebuttal to any smugness about being the leading power in this new mode of conflict followed this line of reasoning: (1) the position of being ahead of one's competitors – measured largely in technological terms – would always be vulnerable to their catching up; (2) the very fact of being "behind" would act to spur others to increase their efforts to catch up; and (3) reaching an arms control agreement would consolidate, for at least a while, one's leadership position. And, beyond the technological realm, there were other aspects of cyberwar, having to do with management of informational resources in ways that could improve military effectiveness, and with the possibility of using the new means of connectivity for waging political warfare. It was my position at the time – a view I still hold all these years later – that the US military was actually falling behind in exploring the implications of advanced information technology for the serious purposes of organizational redesign and military doctrinal innovation. As to subversion and the range of other aspects of "information operations" that fall under a rubric of political warfare, several defense analysts argued that Soviet-era "active measures" practices might in the future work in cyberspace just as well as, if not even better than, they did during the Cold War.[12]

So, when a colleague from the Foreign Military Studies Office at Fort Leavenworth reached out to me in 1995 about the possibility of arranging a meeting

with Russian cyberwar experts, I was intensely interested and, in turn, took the idea to my superiors in
the Office of the Secretary of Defense. At first, the
proposal was dismissed out of hand. But a thoughtful
assistant secretary, overseeing activities then known
as "command, control, communications, and intelligence" (C3I), eventually became a strong advocate
for a meeting whose goal would be, as I was instructed,
to "find out as much as we can about what the Russians
are up to in cyber without telling them too much about
what we are doing."

Even though now blessed with "top cover" provided
by a Pentagon official, the process of gaining the
necessary high-level approval for the meeting proved
arduous. The rules of engagement for the American
team – comprised of a few professors and think-tank
analysts – were onerous, to say the least, regarding
which topics we would be allowed to discuss. It was
refreshing, when the meeting finally took place, over
the course of a week in 1996 – after more than a year
of wrangling – to see how open our Russian counterparts were in their approach to these discussions. But
then there *was* much openness when Boris Yeltsin was
serving as the Russian president.

I did a poor job of policing the American team's
adherence to the rules of engagement – including my
own behavior – as the Russians' clear enthusiasm and
wide-ranging thoughtfulness about all matters cyber
were infectious. For that week, the two teams, a dozen
of us in total, held forth in some of the sharpest (in
the best sense of the word) discussions in which I have
ever participated. The Russians, led by a four-star
admiral, seconded by a three-star flag officer, also
included a lawyer deeply versed in both advanced
technology and international communications agreements, and a number of leading computer scientists.

The group sessions absolutely crackled at each sitting; and my off-line talks with individual Russian delegates were as lively and, in some respects, more informative. The Russians were concerned about technology-oriented matters, but also about the serious potential for American cyberspace-based "influence campaigns" intended to cause chaos in their newly democratizing land. For my part, I was just as concerned that both the technical and the political modes of offensive action that might be taken via cyberspace would soon diffuse and be employed against the United States and other countries around the world. As noted in Chapter 1, I was haunted by visions of a kind of "cool war" – like that first noted and so named in the 1960s by Marshall McLuhan, and then teased out in a novel by Frederik Pohl over a decade later.

To this day, those of us who participated as members of the American team remain bound, for the most part, to confidentiality about the details of the event. But in 2009, *New York Times* reporter John Markoff evidently obtained some information from the Russian side and planned to write about the meeting. He somehow got hold of my name, asked for an interview, and I was given permission to speak with him – with guidance to avoid divulging technical details of the discussions, or even the names of the participants on both sides. It was a level of secrecy that I found counter-productive, but to which I adhered, and to which I still do.

Markoff already had the sense that some detailed technical discussion had taken place; but when he came to me, he correctly focused on what both the Russians and I thought was the single most important issue that had been raised: prospects for cyber arms control. I affirmed this, and told him that a "structural" form of arms control was seen as impossible. This drove us to focus on the possibility of more behavior-based constraints, like those that had made the Chemical and Biological Weapons Conventions possible. I was enthusiastic about this – not only with setting constraints on cyber attacks using worms, viruses, polymorphic engines, and such, but also with the idea that there should be controls in the area of political warfare. Most of my teammates were less sanguine, though few openly opposed such limits.

Serious opposition to cyber arms control came later. When I gave an "after action report" to my superiors in the Pentagon, it was received with a mix of hostility and dismissiveness. The hostility was to the idea that the United States, so far ahead in cyber weaponry and in possession of the world's great media machinery, would somehow willingly agree to refrain from using these powerful tools against a long-time adversary that was seen, as a high-ranking officer put it, as being "on the ropes." As to the possibility of arms control when the principal weaponry was ubiquitous, uncontrollably diffusing information technology, the very notion was dismissed out of hand by those in the room who were far more familiar with the structural form – that is, counting and monitoring weapons – of arms control employed in the nuclear realm. My response was to affirm that our points of advantage over the Russians were a good reason *to engage* in behavioral arms control. For such agreement would consolidate our lead in cyber, and ease Russian fears. I used the example, a favorite of mine, of Winston Churchill's pre-World-War-I offer to Kaiser Wilhelm of a "Naval Holiday" – halting the building of battleships. But the analogy backfired, as one history-minded attendee at the briefing noted that the Kaiser saw the offer as a sign of British weakness, and ramped up the naval arms race. I tried to point out that, this time, the offer came from the lesser power (Russia), not the leader (us). To no avail.

For their part, the Russian team had success with their leadership. Soon their ambassador to the United Nations pushed for an international effort to control the waging of all forms of cyberwar. There was interest among representatives from around the world, leading to General Assembly Resolution 53/70, a document that followed closely the points upon which we had been able to reach agreement during our meeting. However, the US ambassador vetoed the Resolution. Thereafter, Russian diplomats submitted fresh versions of this resolution; each time, the United States, although in nominal support, demurred.[13] John Markoff summed up the situation in his 2009 article, which appeared a week prior to President Obama's visit to Moscow for talks including discussion of cyber matters: "The United States argues that a [cyberwarfare] treaty is unnecessary." Markoff also noted Moscow's concerns, stating that "from the Russian perspective, the absence of a treaty is permitting a kind of arms race with potentially dangerous consequences." He also observed that Moscow was asking for a treaty to "ban a country from secretly embedding malicious codes or circuitry that can be later activated from afar in the event of war."[14]

Needless to say, President Obama's trip to Moscow did not result in any fundamental change regarding cyber arms control. But, by this time, some 13 years after my meeting with the Russians, much had changed. Because there had been no "holiday" in the cyber arms race, the Russians – among others, including China, Iran, and North Korea, to name just a few – had caught up with the United States in cyber technologies. Indeed, as early as the late 1990s, American defense information systems had already been subjected to extended intrusions – code-named Moonlight Maze – that were thought to have been perpetrated by Russian hackers. I had some involvement in this matter, and cannot say more than this; but the long-time cyber "czar" and senior counter-terrorism official Richard Clarke gave a compelling account of Moonlight Maze when he was interviewed on a *PBS Frontline* episode entitled "Cyber War!"[15] I appeared on that episode as well, and arranged for a master hacker of my acquaintance to provide some details about the vulnerability of critical information infrastructures. But that show did little to change policy, or to advance the expert discourse. And soon, a series of apparently China-related intrusions ensued, known as Titan Rain. Theft of intellectual property skyrocketed – and keeps rising. Then cyber political warfare struck in 2016, in ways that still reverberate profoundly.

Given the impossibility of imposing quantitative "structural" controls on advanced information technologies, the only logical alternative left is to craft behavior-based controls on cyber arms. And here the sometimes very positive track record of previous behavioral/operational efforts to control arms racing, improve deterrence, and, at times, ameliorate the destructiveness of war offers hope. It is important to reflect upon earlier such efforts; they may provide useful insights.

Past attempts as prologue to future arms control?

Possessing a particular type of weapon, or perhaps just knowing how to make it, does not imply that it must, should, or inevitably will be regularly employed. For there are times when a weapon is so horrible that, after initial use, it is broadly rejected, even by the worst malefactors. Take mustard gas and other chemical weapons, so widely resorted to during World War I – with hideous effects – that a great antipathy toward them arose, leading to their ban by the Geneva

Convention in 1925. With very few exceptions, this proscription has held ever since. Adolf Hitler, one of a handful of history's most evil characters, was wounded in a gas attack during the Great War, and even he refrained from allowing the use of such weapons in battle during World War II. Despite this, he and his minions *did* employ poison gas against helpless innocents in Nazi death camps, discovery of which added further to the widespread revulsion felt toward chemical weapons. So much so that their rare uses – possibly in the Russo-Afghan and Iraq–Iran conflicts during the 1980s, and in the recent Syrian civil war, among a few other instances – have served only to heighten opposition to them. In 1997, a new Chemical Weapons Convention came into force, and has been embraced and adhered to by nearly 200 countries. In 1972, 25 years earlier, a Biological Weapons Convention was enacted and has had the same level of support.

The interesting point about the chemical and biological agreements to ban such arms is that these are technological areas in which many nations have the wherewithal to develop them. The barriers to entry into this field of weaponry are hardly insurmountable, as basic materials are accessible and the kind of technical skill required exists widely throughout the world. Yet there is overwhelming opposition to developing, stockpiling, or ever using "poison and bugs." And the successful arms control agreements that have helped to keep mankind free of them are based upon a clear willingness of nation-states to self-impose constraints on their own actions. This sort of "behavioral approach" is employed if access to weapons-making materials and related know-how cannot be controlled to any significant extent. In the parlance of arms control, a behavior-based regime is called "operational."

When weapons development is difficult, calling for deep expertise drawn from many disciplines, and rare materials requiring much processing and refining, control strategies are described as "structural." As opposed to more accessible chemical and biological expertise and materials, the nuclear realm is one in which the barriers to entry are far higher, as there is much more ability to control access to fissile material. Added to this, the horrors of the atomic bombings of Hiroshima and Nagasaki provided both ethical and practical impetus for crafting arms control and nonproliferation treaties.

Chemical, biological, and nuclear weapons are all categorized in terms of their capabilities for inflicting mass destruction. It is not at all surprising that efforts to craft operational and/or structural arms control agreements have characterized the world's reactions to them.[16] But what of cyberwar? Bits and bytes may rarely – if increasingly – lead to direct destruction or killing, but cyber weaponry already has the capacity to inflict "mass disruption." Thus, it is important that we explore the possibility now of developing an arms control regime that addresses the rising cyber threat.

From the outset, it seems clear that "structural" arms control will just not prove feasible. Virtually all advanced information technology – which includes the smart, connected, information content and computing power of the billions of items that now form part of the Internet of Things – can be seen as "dual use." That is, a high-performance computer can mine data in search of improving business efficiency, or it can help to break into an enemy system. Your refrigerator can tell you when you need milk, but it can also be hacked, taken under hostile control, and then conscripted into a robot army that launches a major infrastructure attack. There is simply no way to maintain tight rein over the fundamental building blocks of cyberwar.

Given the relative ease of access to highly disruptive capabilities, is it at all reasonable to posit the rise of a voluntary system of self-control that would keep nations – and perhaps even some non-state actors – from waging cyberwar? The record of similar types of efforts is not promising, especially the case of emergent strategic air power a century ago. From the time H. G. Wells published his novel *The War in the Air* in 1908, the idea of bringing an adversary nation to its knees via aerial bombardment has captured the imagination of military strategists, political leaders, and mass publics. The Great War saw the first such campaign, with German Zeppelins and Gotha bombers hitting at Britain from the air. Material damage done was small; but postwar improvements in aircraft speed, range, and payload-carrying capacity generated a fear that, as three-time British Prime Minister Stanley Baldwin said in 1932, "The bomber will always get through."[17] Acceptance of this idea led to efforts to ban strategic bombing. Even hyper-aggressive Adolf Hitler, as George Quester noted, "was extremely reluctant to have his own population centers bombed."[18] So, during the 1938 Munich crisis, Hitler went so far as to forbid his Luftwaffe from targeting Czech cities.[19]

Hitler's self-restraint was remarkable, given that his decision to speed up German rearmament – and reject the constraints of the Versailles Treaty – had led to the dissolution in 1934 of the World Disarmament Conference held under the auspices of the League of Nations. That Conference had been able to achieve much progress, with France agreeing to limit bomber activity to use against invading foreign forces – to help drive them from French soil – and Britain calling for a multilateral end to the expansion of air forces.[20] In the event, the failure of the Conference led to an aerial arms race, but it did *not* lead to an embrace of the idea of bombing cities. Though air power was a leading element in the first ground combat operations of World War II in Poland and France, some sense of behavior-based constraint remained.

George Quester summed up the situation well: "Despite the many dire prewar predictions of a terroristic conflict, leaving no sanctuary for civilian populations . . . the opening rounds of World War II now witnessed no bombing raids at all on the populated areas of Britain and France or of Germany."[21] Sadly, this was not true of Warsaw and Rotterdam, both of which were heavily bombed in 1939 and 1940, respectively. London's turn came next and, for the following five years, cities were bombed and civilians incinerated with deliberate fury.

The targeting of noncombatants from the air continued after World War II. The Korean War, erupting just five years later, saw just as relentless bombing campaigns by the United Nations forces deployed in that conflict. Virtually every single building in the North Korean capital, Pyongyang, was leveled by aerial bombardment. Hanoi and many smaller cities – and even villages – were subjected to similar treatment during the Vietnam War that came next. In both cases, it was to little avail. As Max Hastings said about the use of strategic bombing in Korea, "belief in 'victory through air power' was put to the test and found wanting."[22] That war ended in a costly stalemate. But the result in Vietnam was far worse for the side so reliant on aerial bombing; the American-led effort ended in a communist take-over of South Vietnam.

Perhaps this is why a kind of tacit agreement seems to have emerged after the fall of Saigon in 1975: there has been no mass-destructive aerial bombing campaign since. For its part, the US Air Force has focused on waging far more discriminate campaigns. To be sure, NATO's air war against Serbia in 1999 and the American-led "shock and awe" bombing of Iraq four years later were extensive, but both efforts strove to limit civilian casualties. This emerging pattern of self-restraint may indicate that reining in cyberwar as a mode of "strategic attack" could possibly be feasible too.

In the case of air power, there is today no formal, behavior-based treaty – like those sought in the 1930s, but which quickly came undone in the crucible of World War II, when the threat of strategic bombing lacked the ability to deter the outbreak of armed conflict in the first place. Thus, it seems problematic to try to tie "operational arms control" efforts to a notion of deterrence. For, as soon as deterrence fails, any inhibition about using the deterrent weapon itself fades – especially if the weapon is believed to have real military utility. No, it seems that abhorrence is necessary in order to cultivate self-restraint. This was certainly the case with chemical weapons after World War I. And it appears to be so with the horrors associated with germ warfare as well. Even aerial bombing seems to have gone too far in its many applications – though its lack of effectiveness as a strategic tool, a key point observed by Robert Pape,[23] may have played a role in the cessation of efforts to level cities from the air. As to nuclear weapons, it would be most comforting to say that militaries and their leaders find them repellent; but the fact that nuclear deterrence has been and remains dependent upon the stated willingness to target civilians – the euphemism for this particular brutality is "counter-value targeting" – gives pause. And suggests deterrence is just too slender a reed to rely upon as a basis for operational cyber arms control.

Yet there is something paradoxical, manifested in the 1972 Anti-Ballistic Missile Treaty between the United

States and the Soviet Union, suggesting a willingness to engage in operational arms control – in this case mutual agreement to forgo building serious defenses – so as to shore up deterrence by continuing to hold civilian populations at risk. This agreed-upon forbearance, the experts at Stanford University's Arms Control Group noted, meant "each country renounced the right to build certain defenses. Such a renunciation is unprecedented."[24] The basic logic of maintaining a "balance of terror" was that uneven progress in fielding effective defenses would give one side or the other offensive advantages, creating instability and pressure to develop sufficient missiles to overwhelm even robust defenses.

For 30 years, both Washington and Moscow adhered to the ABM Treaty – a most meaningful product of the first Strategic Arms Limitations Talks (SALT I) – until the time when President George W. Bush announced the American intention to withdraw. This was something that not even Ronald Reagan, an advocate of building missile defenses, was willing to do. There is reason to be concerned about the search for missile defenses – still elusive to this day – sparking a new arms race in offensive weapons. But if mutual restraint is possible in the high-stakes nuclear arena, perhaps there is hope for cyber too.

A major difference, though, is that strategic cyberwar features none of the horrors of weapons of mass destruction, and is increasingly thought to be able to achieve the kinds of effects against infrastructure that bombardment from the air can – but with bits and bytes rather than bombs and missiles, engendering far less physical destruction and greatly reducing the likelihood of sparking moral outrage. In short, strategic cyber attack appears to be a far more usable option. The question therefore may be: why would any nation *refrain* from employing a cyber mode of attack? And the possibility that such attacks might be mounted anonymously, across a range of situations falling below the level of open warfare between known combatants, only seems to reinforce the notion that strategic cyber attack is a usable option.

An interesting historical analogy highlighting the problem posed when a weapon or tactic ostensibly has high "usability" when there is ambiguity as to the identity of the perpetrator – but perhaps contains some risks as well – arose during the Spanish Civil War (1936–9), when convoys of Soviet ships sailed across the Mediterranean to deliver supplies to the beleaguered Republican forces. Along with Germany, Italy supported Spain's fascist "nationalists," and began a secret campaign with its submarines to torpedo Russian ships. Losses to the supply ships mounted quickly. When accused, the Italians said, "The attacks must have been conducted by pirates." The British, who favored the Republicans, would have none of this, and told the Italians they would be held responsible for any further "pirate attacks." This warning was delivered at a conference in Nyon, Switzerland, in the autumn of 1937, which Winston Churchill recalled was "brief and successful," and "the outrages stopped at once."[25] So it seems that there may be times when even a veil of anonymity proves insufficient to avoid retaliatory acts.

The example from the Spanish Civil War may provide some impetus for efforts to impose behavior-based controls on violent action in conditions other than of direct, open warfare between two parties or contending sets of allies. The point is that, if the identity of a perpetrator is *known*, even if evidence to prove culpability is lacking, remedial or punitive action can still be threatened or taken. As was the case, for example, just a month after the American presidential election of November 2016, when President Barack Obama, still in office, imposed economic sanctions on Russia for having interfered in the electoral process via cyberspace-based political warfare. Despite a lack of "courtroom quality" evidence then, action was still taken.[26]

Firm responses of this sort, or like the strong British position taken against Italian submarine operations in 1937, should point out the costs and risks of covert actions of these sorts, and create at least some openness of mind to notions of reaching mutually agreed-upon behavioral controls. And it should be noted that operational arms control need not be perfect, either, in terms of keeping the peace entirely. Indeed, this type of constraint should be seen as an element of military strategy. This point was made compellingly, long ago, by Thomas Schelling and Morton Halperin in their classic study, *Strategy and Arms Control*. They put the matter this way:

> We believe that arms control is a promising, but still only dimly perceived, enlargement of the scope of military strategy. It rests essentially on the recognition that our military relation with potential enemies is not one of pure conflict and opposition, but involves strong elements of mutual interest in the avoidance of a war that neither side wants, in minimizing the costs and risks of the arms competition, and in curtailing the scope and violence of war in the event it occurs.[27]

In their view, arms control is an integral part of military strategy. I would take it a step further and contend that, given the high politics and diplomacy involved – and the economic benefits of avoiding costly arms spirals – the idea of agreeing upon mutual controls is actually a key aspect of grand strategy. This highest level of statecraft, where suasion and the shadow of force are omnipresent and intertwined, has seen striking successes of behavior-based efforts at arms control, as in the instances of the aforementioned chemical and biological weapons conventions. Even threats of nuclear annihilation have lost much of their ominous presence in our lives, given that treaties aimed at reductions that were first negotiated in the 1980s and built upon – e.g., the START process – are still mostly adhered to today.

That said, there has long been serious skepticism about the possibility of reaching durable arms control agreements, particularly those that rely on willingly self-imposed behavioral constraints. For example, in 1912, Alfred Thayer Mahan, the American apostle of preponderant sea power, saw arms competitions as productive "investments" that fostered prosperity by acting to "shield industries and commerce." Besides, he went on to argue, force was truly the principal tool of statecraft: "For in diplomacy, in international negotiation, force underlies *every* contention as a possible final arbiter, and of force war is simply the ultimate expression."[28] The following year, when Winston Churchill – then First Lord of the Admiralty – proposed that lasting peace between Britain and Germany could be achieved by declaring a "Naval Holiday" in the building of dreadnought (all-big-gun) battleships,[29] Kaiser Wilhelm declined the offer of this behavior-based arms control proposal, basing his decision on "manly, and (*sic*) unaffrighted maintenance of our own interests ... I shall go on ruthlessly and implacably."[30] He did. The arms race continued, and the Great War broke out the following year.

The cautionary tale of Churchill and the Kaiser had a coda in World War I, when the Germans chose to violate the international norms of naval warfare by having their U-boats operate in "unrestricted" fashion – that is, striking without warning, leading to great loss of life among those on stricken merchant ships. Having tried at the outset of the war to use their submarines in restrained ways by stopping targeted vessels and giving warning and time for crews and passengers to get into lifeboats, the Germans found that doing so put their submarines at greater risk and slowed the rate of sinkings. Thus, an agreed-upon behavioral constraint on the waging of this form of naval warfare fell prey to the severe – and, as the war dragged on, increasing – demands of "strategic necessity."

In the wake of a series of incidents that resulted in significant numbers of deaths at sea among neutrals – as with the sinking of the *Lusitania* – the Germans were briefly chastened, but then returned to unrestricted submarine warfare and ultimately caused the United States to join the fight on the side of the Allies. Interestingly, it was rising moral outrage at the violations of international norms, to which Germany had agreed before the war, that drove much of the American fervor to enter the conflict. As historian A. A. Hoehling observed, "Preachers almost everywhere extolled the virtues of a 'holy crusade.'"[31] So, in this case, as with the Kaiser's failure to accept the Naval Holiday proposal, rejection of a behavioral constraint proved highly counter-productive in the end. Similar risks may attend the rejection of any behavior-based control proposals aimed at limiting depredations that may be committed via cyberspace. The differences between the actions of U-boats and cyber bots may not be as great as they seem.

Moving from the cautionary to the hopeful, one can find in recent air campaigns sustained efforts to avoid civilian losses. And in the fact that, since Hiroshima and Nagasaki in 1945, nuclear weapons have never again been used in anger – despite their substantial proliferation and the spate of wars, hot and cold, that have bedeviled the world ever since. As to the American "massive retaliation" doctrine adopted in the 1950s, which held that *any* act of aggression could be responded to with nuclear weapons, it was seen by allies, enemies, and the whole world community as utterly outrageous and unjustifiable on any legal or moral grounds. Thomas Schelling summed up the folly of this policy quite succinctly: "Massive retaliation was a doctrine in decline from its enunciation in 1954."[32] The doctrine soon died a quiet death, a sign that behavior-based constraints were possible even in the realm of weapons of mass destruction. Might such limits arise as well to deal with mass disruption? I have always sought to answer this query affirmatively.

Did the United States unwittingly spark the ongoing cyber arms race?

The sad irony of the American opposition to cyber arms control is that the position of leadership the United States once enjoyed in technical aspects of cyberspace-based operations has been lost. Russia and China have come close to pulling level with the United States in offensive capabilities; and Moscow's and Beijing's cyber minions have provided them with superior defenses. Aside from Russia and China, in Richard Clarke and Robert Knake's expert views, Iran and North Korea have leapt past the United States in cyber defensive capabilities.[33] So it seems that the Pentagon's argument for refraining from joining a behavior-based arms control regime because, as was thought, "We're ahead" has proved hollow – and counter-productive.

Yet it must be recognized that there was a time when the United States had a substantial lead across the spectrum of cyberwar capabilities. And professional militaries, not to mention political leaders to whom they answer – when governance is by other than military juntas – are loath to cede or constrain any superiority that they may enjoy. This was the case in the 1960s, when General Curtis LeMay took the position that US nuclear superiority was not a threat to others, and needed to be sustained. As he put the matter so starkly, "America, even with a distinct superiority, does not need to be deterred from waging war. On the other hand, decreasing American superiority can create a precarious military imbalance."[34]

This was an understandable attitude, but one that only spurred the Russians to ever greater efforts to achieve at least nuclear parity with the United States. Thankfully, an unending nuclear arms race was avoided, replaced by a preference for seeking arms control agreements. Given that the cyber situation is one in which an initial American position of leadership has already been superseded, one can only hope that a willingness to engage in arms control will replace LeMay-style intransigence.

It is well past time for the United States, which has been the principal obstructionist of cyber arms control at the United Nations, to embrace the opportunity to craft a behavior-based ban on use of the virtual domain for purposes of engaging in covert economic and political warfare, and to tamp down the urge to go beyond espionage by utilizing intrusions for purposes of preparing the way for acts of strategic cyber attack. All of the behaviors that a cyber arms control agreement would prohibit are, in some respects, like acts of war. It is already well understood in international law that striking at an opponent's economy by naval blockade or commerce raiding creates a state of armed conflict. Cyber theft of the vital intellectual property that undergirds the dynamism and competitiveness of an economy should be seen in a similar light. The same goes for cybotage, which should be seen as equivalent to placing explosives in key places – except that insertion of malicious bits and bytes is likely to have wider, more disruptive effects.

Cyberspace-based political warfare – whether aimed at subverting democracy *or* at overthrowing authoritarians – should be a matter upon which agreement is easily reached. It was certainly an issue of great concern to the Russians at our 1996 meeting, when their early efforts to democratize were fragile. And it is an issue in the United States and other liberal societies today – they worry about the possibilities of mass audiences being duped by phonied-up propaganda, computer-enhanced "deep fake" videos, and more.

Overall, the reasons to strive for behavior-based arms control in many cyber-related areas – e.g., infrastructure attacks, theft of intellectual property, and political mischief making – are compelling. Obstacles to agreement in these areas hardly seem insurmountable. The only dimension of cyberwar that would fall outside the realm of behavior-based control would be strictly military, as the evolution of warfare toward the *Bitskrieg* paradigm simply cannot be prevented – including the increasing integration of robots into the whole strategic apparatus of nations. The face of battle has always been reshaped by technological advances; and since *Bitskrieg*, like its forebear *Blitzkrieg*, aims at mass disruption to enable short, sharp combat operations – less bloody ones, too – this aspect of cyberwar will not be controllable.

Could a behavior-based cyber arms control agreement really work?

As noted above, there have been serious failures in earlier attempts to craft behavior-based limits on the use of weapons that are either already diffusing or (relatively) easy to make. Winston Churchill's attempt to call a "holiday" in the Anglo-German naval arms race prior to World War I actually seems to have emboldened Kaiser Wilhelm, with ultimately disastrous results. Then there were the sincere multilateral efforts in the 1920s and 1930s to come to an agreement that civilian populations would not be deliberately targeted for aerial bombardment. A hint of looming future failures was provided by the devastating air attack on Guernica during the Spanish Civil War. Then, from even early on in World War II, all pretense of sparing civilians the ordeal of aerial bombing was dropped, culminating in the annihilating attacks on Hiroshima and Nagasaki in 1945 that ushered in the Nuclear Age.

But sometimes, even in failure the seeds of success can be glimpsed. No atomic weapon has been detonated in anger since 1945, despite the many thousands of warheads in the arsenals of the world's various nuclear-armed powers. Conventional air attack on civilian targets has also become less common, especially in recent decades. Chemical and biological weapons have been outlawed internationally. These are all good things.

Clearly, there are conditions under which behavior-based arms control – achieved by either formal agreements or tacit norms – can work sustainably. It is easy to see why chemical and biological weapons have been so widely rejected: they are hideous. But what are the prospects when a weapon is of a much less odious nature, and aims at disruption rather than at destruction? A good example of behavior-based controls on weapons that don't aim to kill people would be the Treaty on Principles Governing the Activities of States in the Exploration and Use of Outer Space, Including the Moon and Other Celestial Bodies – known more simply as the "Outer Space Treaty" – in force since 1967. The Treaty seeks to limit weaponization of outer space; yet, as journalist James Canan noted, this restriction "applies [primarily] to nuclear weapons. But it leaves moot the legality of conventional explosives in space."[35] For many decades, this loophole was not exploited, in part due to lack of technologies for fighting in space, but also because of increasing reliance of advanced countries upon the smooth functioning of space-based communications. Now, though, an outer space arms race is under way, with the new US Space Force and other nations' emerging weapons capabilities providing signs that behavior-based controls are under growing pressure.[36]

A war in outer space would be immensely disruptive to the world's economies, the social interactions of countless peoples, and, increasingly, to the ability of military organizations to function and fight effectively. Yet the behavioral basis for keeping conflict from "reaching orbit" – so to speak – is losing its power to dissuade. Perhaps the explanation here has to do with technological determinism. Emerging technologies now make it easier to fight in outer space. But this reasoning fails against the fact that, from early on, both sides in the Cold War had space weaponry to aim at satellites, from American "miniature homing vehicles" (MHV) to Russian "super grenades." Blinding or destroying orbital assets has always been easier than putting them *in* orbit. So, perhaps restraint has been more ethically than technically driven. President Jimmy Carter, for example, took the view that it was in the world's interest – thus imposing an obligation on the United States in its role as leader of the free nations – to seek "maximum pacification of space."[37] Carter supported the complete demilitarization of outer space; but he was aware of others' weapons and concluded, "the United States finds itself under increasing pressure to field an anti-satellite capability of its own."[38]

Could the example of this longstanding effort to impose and sustain behavior-based controls on conflict in outer space inform an initiative that might aim at doing the same for cyberspace? One way to see this analogy would be to say that, by comparison, mutual restraint will likely erode more swiftly in cyberspace because the ability to mount attacks – of many varied types – is much easier to achieve in the virtual domain than it is in outer space. But the fact that there are now a variety of ways to wage war against satellites, ranging from the disruptive to the destructive, and still we see no attacks on them, is a sign that, in the absence of open armed conflict, there is little benefit in mounting such assaults in so-called "peacetime." A kind of self-deterrence prevails, no doubt in part because of the solemn pledges the more than 100 signatories of the Outer Space Treaty have made to each other.[39] Some may be engaged in an arms race in space weaponry, but they are most unlikely to employ these capabilities unless the stakes are seen as being sufficiently high to merit their use in acts of open warfare. This is quite similar to the case with cyber weaponry, where equally swift advances have been made in development of malicious software able to disrupt computer networks with potentially grave economic, military, or sociopolitical effects. Yet, absent open warfare, some degree of self-deterrence applies here, too.

The analogy between existing behavior-based arms control in outer space and the potential for a similar sort of agreement to limit cyber conflict is hardly perfect. But there is enough, in the long "orbital peace" overseen – and in part sustained – by the Outer Space Treaty, to embark on a similar venture in cyberspace. Indeed, if a Cyberspace Treaty were to last for over half a century, it would more than justify its having been reached in the first place. But the Outer Space

Treaty may go on longer, with even those armed to the teeth with orbital weaponry unwilling to use their arsenals, unless *in extremis*, and in the context of a broader period of open conflict. The same may well hold were a cyber arms control agreement to be reached.

One might logically ask, then, "If there will be cyber self-deterrence, as there seems to be in outer space, why is a cyber arms control agreement necessary?" A simple answer is that a formal agreement establishes clear norms of behavior to which countries bind themselves. It is why there have been so many different kinds of arms control agreements – for biological, chemical, and nuclear weapons, conventional weapons, both offensive and defensive missile systems, incidents at sea, and more – in so many areas where nations already behave with self-restraint. The very act of agreeing upon such norms of behavior reinforces and sustains the willingness to act in continuing compliance. Such affirmation breeds "behavioral confirmation."

And it legitimately raises the stakes for scofflaws when they are caught in the act of debasing the values to which they have so formally sworn allegiance. In the case of war in outer space, the attacker's identity would almost surely become known immediately – perhaps even while the attack was under way. While the same is hardly true when it comes to cyberspace-based attacks, the forensics in this field have seen major improvements since David Ronfeldt and I first developed the cyberwar concept back in the early 1990s. The risk of getting caught in – or soon after – the act has only grown.

But, beyond practical risk–return calculations – the "hard currency" of classical *Realpolitik* – behavior-based international norms establish patterns of interaction that provide a foundation for steady, ongoing, and reliable relations, even between adversaries. Such behavioral "regimes" (the term of art), as Robert Axelrod and Robert Keohane have asserted, "do not enforce rules in a hierarchical sense, but they do change patterns of transaction costs and provide information to participants, so that uncertainty is reduced."[40] Perhaps the greatest benefit a behavior-based cyber arms control agreement can provide is simply to reduce, to an appreciable degree, the uncertainty that accompanies persistent conditions of stark, well-armed hostility.

Nevertheless, there are pragmatic matters to take into consideration. Treaties take time to negotiate, sign, and ratify. The conventions covering biological and chemical weapons took years to articulate, then put into effect. But without taking the behavioral/operational approach to arms control, reaching these agreements would have been impossible. For too many countries have the capability to develop biological and chemical weapons. Far too many technologies would have to be curtailed, monitored, and verified. The same goes for technologies associated with cyberwar. Almost all information technologies have to be considered "dual use" – that is, they can be used for either civilian or military purposes. The classic "structural" approach to arms control is simply impossible, a situation that is much in line with technological trends that have been emerging for the past several decades. Albert Legault made this point powerfully – an insight relevant to cyber concerns today – in his early study of the spread of advanced missiles:

> Many items that were uncontrolled in the past can today have military applications. Moreover, the increasing tendency of civilian industry to adopt ever more sophisticated technologies makes it all the more difficult to control goods and know-how deemed to be "dual-use" – that is, to have both military and civilian applications.

To control such items would require much tighter regulations, with related administrative and bureaucratic complications – to say nothing of the negative effect upon economic interests in the affected states.[41]

And, it must be noted, even the strong norms of behavior that animated and sustained the Missile Technology Control Regime (MTCR) reached in 1987 under the aegis of the G-7, to which a total of nearly three dozen advanced countries have adhered, have come under great pressure due to technological advances. Indeed, in this instance, it is a cyber factor that threatens to upset the equilibrium: the use of highly advanced artificial intelligence not only to guide hypersonic missiles, but to do so in-flight in ways that respond to evolving operational changes and adversary defensive countermeasures. At present, the leaders in this area are Russia and China. The United States made its first Mach 5 missile test in March 2020. For the present, there is little interest among the "hypersonic powers" in diffusing this technology more widely; but, if the historical pattern of technological advances holds, the world will likely see the spread of this weapon system, whose speed and maneuver capabilities are so greatly enhanced by the machine-learning process that keeps improving the skills – at hyper speed – of its robotic "pilot." The only way to deal with them may be to craft a defensive system run by *other* robots. As journalist Kristina Lindborg has put the matter of how to defend against hypersonics, "Only complex AI-based sensor systems are capable of detecting and intercepting them."[42]

This brings us back to the matter, first mentioned in Chapter 1, of efforts at the United Nations to forbid development of Lethal Autonomous Weapons Systems (LAWS). Should a behavior-based cyber arms control treaty embrace this effort to ban weaponized robots? In my view, doing so would admit to prejudice against silicon-based intelligence, as well as more generally against advances in machine technology. Besides, the basic reason to pursue behavior-based, "operational" arms control in cyber is that there is no way to limit the development, production, and diffusion of information technologies that are almost all dual use. This tide cannot be stemmed.

Another difficulty with the UN LAWS initiative is that it does not outlaw robots that provide intelligence, surveillance, and reconnaissance (ISR), yet these bots are already used with lethal effect in counter-terrorist and other operations. They don't shoot, but they do identify and guide those who do, greatly enhancing the lethality of human trigger-pullers. A great example of how robotic ISR systems can improve the lethality of human soldiers was provided in a field exercise at Fort Benning in 2019, when a heavily outnumbered small force absolutely decimated its opponents thanks to its entirely robotized ISR system – one that the "enemy" did not have.[43]

The Fort Benning exercise is just one more example of how robotics will likely change the future face of battle. As to already existing weaponry, attempts to outlaw these "lethal autonomous" systems might require the elimination of such weapons as, for example, the Tomahawk land-attack missile (TLAM), in use for decades, which *is* a robot. The only "human in the loop" has to do with the initial decision to launch a TLAM – the same level of control that exists over more recent robotic weapons, and that will continue to guide the deployment of future robotic weapons systems. No, there cannot be a way to purge militaries of all lethal robots – from weapons to ISR systems that then guide other deadly munitions. One might just as well try to eliminate tanks, planes, or aircraft carriers. Robots that will fight in open battle are going to be serving regularly alongside human soldiers, sailors, and airmen – and the nations that field them should indeed be held responsible for any actions of AI Jane that may violate the laws of war.

What part of cyber weaponry, then, is left to be subject to operational, behavior-based arms control? In my view, there are two main areas that can and should be made subject to limitations: the use of cyber for purposes of waging political warfare, and as a means of mounting "strategic attacks" on civilian infrastructures. These are the areas that the Russians and I agreed to pursue when we met back in 1996 – which the US government has blocked.

But American opposition has not been completely steadfast. President Barack Obama, as previously mentioned, reached out to President Xi in the hope of reaching a behavior-based Sino-American accord, by the terms of which each country would pledge to refrain from attacking the other's critical infrastructures during peacetime. I credit Leon Panetta with providing strong support for engaging in this form of arms control. I have worked with Mr. Panetta on cyber matters over the past two decades, and have found his insights in this area deeply thoughtful. That said, the "peacetime" phrasing of the Obama cyber initiative is still a sticking point, given that a war could be *started* with such an attack. So I have always tried to use the analogy of air power, and the long effort to refrain from indiscriminate attacks on civilians – which dominated the early discourse a century ago, was violated from World War II through Vietnam, but which seems finally to have taken hold. Why not rid ourselves of the "peacetime" limitation on controlling cyber attacks on infrastructure? And, instead, covenant not to launch attacks on targets which will primarily affect civilians *at any time.* This would still allow *Bitskrieg* to unfold in battle, but the threat of "mass disruption" of civilian societies would be avoided. A good thing.

I first proposed this form of behavior-based cyber arms control in an article in 1999, making the case that the strictures of "just war" theory, from Thomas Aquinas to Hugo Grotius – and beyond – have always affirmed the requirement to maintain the immunity of noncombatants. It is but a short step to extend this line of thinking from the protection of civilians' lives to the technological systems upon which their lives so increasingly depend. I went on further, noting that adherence to what is ethical could also have very practical benefits, given that "whoever might begin the business of striking at civilian-oriented targets [by cyber means] invites retaliation in kind – both from nation-states and from individuals or small groups that are armed with advanced information technological capabilities."[44] Given that liberal, open, developed societies – such as the United States and most of its allies and friends – are the most vulnerable to cyber attacks on infrastructure, as well as to the cyber-based forms of political warfare that have emerged in recent years, it would seem that behavior-based arms control should be pursued with some sense of urgency.

The same applies to some of the other strategic implications of this period of technological change that will be considered in the concluding chapter.

5

Through a Screen Darkly

Given the extent to which lives are increasingly lived, commerce conducted, and conflicts sparked online, the availability and security of connectivity, and the authenticity and timeliness of messages are of paramount, increasing importance. As are the growing effects of what begins in, and then emerges from, cyberspace on the broader course of events in the physical world – from social mobilization movements to shooting wars. Statecraft, strategy, and diplomacy may also be largely reshaped by advances in information technologies – including by automation, if not yet by a full-blown version of artificial intelligence. In short, the world is at an inflection point as great as the one wrought by the onset of the last major era of technological advances, the Industrial Revolution, but one that is even more complex in our time. With this in mind, I focus herein on a set of pressing challenges that, should they be dealt with effectively, hold out the promise of greater prosperity and more durable peace. Should they remain unmet, an ever more discontented, disrupted, even chaotic world will form our global future.

Rethinking cybersecurity

Much evidence was presented in the first two chapters of this book to make the point that, by any set of reasonable measures, the existing framework for cyber-security, primarily based on the twin pillars of firewalls and antiviral software, has proved insufficient to protect private citizens, businesses, and other key institutions of society and governance. Hundreds of millions of people around the world have been hacked, and intel-lectual property worth trillions of dollars has been stolen. Classified information systems have, too, often been breached, undermining the security of a range of nations and their military and intelligence branches. The Internet of Things has emerged, now posing the prospect that intelligent, interconnected cars and many household appliances can be mustered into the ranks of malicious robot networks – by the *billions* – giving even simple DDoS techniques vast new power. And the fact that critical infrastructures in many countries, including "developed" nations such as the United States, were built prior to the creation of the Net and the Web, yet are connected to them, opens up whole new frontiers of risk, given that power grids and pipelines were not engineered with connectivity of this sort in mind. Thus, we are challenged to rethink cybersecurity.

As suggested in Chapter 2, a shift of emphasis toward ubiquitous use of strong encryption and Cloud computing – instead of over-reliance on anti-virals and firewalls – is urgently needed. But there is a larger question that must be asked, and which may require just as much willingness to engage in paradigm-busting:

who provides cybersecurity? Clearly, in liberal societies, the generally open market systems have failed to encourage companies in the private sector to design and sell a range of the most secure and strongly encrypted products. Governments of these societies, with few exceptions, are hamstrung by impediments from both political Right and Left, with concerns about loss of privacy and other possible intrusions upon individual civil liberties crippling legislative efforts to provide cybersecurity while still serving the needs of law enforcement. Hampered by pressures from their constituencies, elected officials have, for the most part, proved unable to address rising threats posed to the people, commerce, and – as seen in the Russian intrusion into the American elections in 2016 – even to the quality of political discourse. In authoritarian states, governments are uninhibited by policy constraints imposed by their publics, and have crafted very strong defensive systems, imposing virtual "border controls" on cyberspace – along with more intrusive methods of social control. But without such recourse to executive *Diktat*, or sweeping cybersecurity legislation, what are the world's liberal societies to do? Staying wide open to cyber attack is not an option.

The solution to this problem can be found, I believe, in the people of liberal societies themselves. The gifted, talented few with the ability to make strong encryption widely available have on occasion outflanked governmental control efforts, as Steven Levy recounted in his compelling tale of the American "code rebels."[1] But availability of a solution provided by an elite few does not by itself determine the pace and extent of a diffusion process. To this day, decades after the success of the code rebels, American cybersecurity remains in an exceptionally poor state – as does that of many other liberal societies. So, the issue now has to do with how mass publics can be encouraged to adopt the best approaches to cybersecurity. If we want to ensure that people around the world will embrace better protection by the adoption of the strongest types of encryption and by making efficient use of Cloud computing, we must ask: "How is this to be achieved?"

To my mind, the answer to this challenge can be found in the classic work on diffusion of organizational forms, new tools, and practices by the sociologist Everett Rogers. In his accounts of the spread of kinder-gartens as an educational concept and wide adoption of the best agricultural practices – among other innova-tions – Rogers found that diffusion processes were quite profoundly shaped by the social systems in which they were nested. He believed that the varied proclivities of a people would ultimately determine whether, and at what pace, a particular institutional form, tool, or practice would diffuse among the members of a given society.[2]

What might this mean, I have long pondered, for my own American society? Here, even in a nation comprised so largely of immigrants from the four corners of the world, a key may be found in the notion that Americans are either imbued with, or quickly develop, the self-reliant traits that form the over-arching ethos that comes with the idea – first artic-ulated by the historian Frederick Jackson Turner – that they are a "frontier people." Americans have been, he argued in a speech to the American Historical Association in 1893, "compelled to adapt themselves to the changes of an expanding people . . . involved in crossing a continent, in winning a wilderness." He went on to say, of frontiers, that they are "the outer edge of the wave" of civilization, and that they not only are reshaped by the civilized, but evoke deep changes in those who would strive to tame these wild spaces.[3] Not least in the form of imposing a norm of self-reliance upon those who would dwell and seek to prosper in such environments. Frontier folk grow accustomed to the idea of having to provide for their own security, and that government may not be able to respond quickly or effectively enough to protect them at "the outer edge." As the late cyber libertarian John Perry Barlow noted, cyberspace is just such an edge, which he labeled the "electronic frontier."

Cyberspace is a place where the hand of governance remains light, where law enforcement, at best, exists in patches, and where international cooperation against crime, terrorism, and militancy is still in its formative stages of development. All the evidence of malign acts in cyberspace over the past several decades – counting, say, from the 1988 Morris Worm – suggests that little state-level progress has been made in protecting people, commercial enterprises, even governmental and military entities, from the depredations of those who move swiftly and with ease throughout the virtual wilderness. It is much like the example of the American West in the nineteenth century, of which Turner wrote so eloquently. There, the pioneering settlers were preyed upon relentlessly, as were banks, stagecoach lines, and other businesses. Even US military presence was, for years at a time, forced to withdraw from what General S. L. A. Marshall described as the "crimsoned prairie."[4] Those who remained were hardy and, yes, self-reliant. But they also worked together, creating local systems of rapid response to emerging threats – whether from Indians or outlaws. The analogy with cyberspace, in self-reliant terms, would be today for all to make extensive use of strong encryption. As to collective action, the notion of forming cyber militias fits very well, along the lines of the Estonian model mentioned in Chapter 2.

As with all analogies, the notion of cyberspace being like a frontier zone in the physical world has its limits. "Real" frontiers – whatever their size – tend to be reduced as they are settled, cultivated, ultimately tamed. But cyberspace is a wilderness that continues to grow, faster than the rate of "settlement" of some of its areas. Expansion of the virtual domain creates many fresh ungoverned spaces, affording new jumping-off points for those who would raid already settled areas – to steal their intellectual property, "kidnap" data and hold it for ransom, engage in other forms of commercial extortion, and perhaps even try, via political warfare, to upset the basic processes of governance, particularly in the liberal societies of the world.

These limitations of the frontier analogy in no way devalue the importance of encouraging the "hardiness" of those increasingly living their lives online. Self-reliance via strong encryption, and collective action in the form of local cyber militias, are both essential. But it is clear that something more is needed to protect society and security in cyberspace – something only governments are able to provide. In the American West of the nineteenth century, tough pioneers blazed paths of settlement and civilization; but the many persistent threats they had to deal with could not be eliminated without skillful military action as well – attuned to the irregular strategic and tactical conditions of fighting elusive enemies across expansive, unsettled terrain.

Thus, there is a pressing need to learn to operate in, and to some extent to tame, the virtual wilderness. There are two basic ways to do this. One, discussed above, is about improving the self-defensive capabilities of those – people, commercial enterprises, and institutional entities – who are settling, or are already settled, in cyberspace. But there is another, more proactive, approach that should also be cultivated. It has to do with learning to detect, track, and disrupt the criminals, terrorists, and militants whose networks remain vibrant, and who continue to pose vital threats, who not only act in the less settled areas of cyberspace but also have the ability to raid from them and strike virtually anywhere. Here the frontier analogy meets a partner: the idea that present-day cyber criminals, terrorists, and militants are like the types of bandits who flourished for many centuries throughout the physical world – and persist even today in some poorly governed spaces. Bandits can come from the chronically poor, who engage in brigandage out of survival instincts. Others, such as the medieval Cult of the Assassins, commit crimes but are driven by religious zealotry. Then there are "noble robbers," who seek to overthrow oppression (the Robin Hood legend is archetypal).[5]

Cyberspace is replete with banditry driven by *all* of these sorts of motivations. The virtual domain is an environment riven by countless small- and startling large-scale acts of theft, bitter persecutions of those deemed to be "the other," and political warfare waged against an ever-widening number of democratic societies. Some few who fall in the last category, those with political motivations, might be considered noble robbers who seek, via theft and subsequent revelation of corrupt secrets of the powerful, to inform and empower those exploited by elites. Julian Assange fits this particular mold, given his support for efforts to "out" over-intrusive surveillance methods, the rigging of political nomination processes, and other acts of malfeasance. But the darker forms of cyber banditry far outweigh the "noble" part of this spectrum of virtual behavior. And the fact that many miscreant hackers are closely tied to nation-states – often acting as their surrogates – only stiffens the challenge. Those who opt to align with nations, as the Internet Research Agency has with Russia, have found the way, as Hobsbawm put it, to "enter the world of real power themselves." In his survey, Hobsbawm saw that the bandits who persisted over time generally linked up with a state sponsor. As he concluded, "in the last analysis they had to come to terms with whatever centers of superior power were prepared to tolerate them, or go under."[6]

Given that the Information Age has enabled a cyber-rebirth of the many forms of banditry – which often render dark service to nations that are willing to employ them – a critical question now is, "How are depredations of this sort to be curtailed?" The mostly defensive paradigm pursued over the past 30-plus years has proved inadequate. But even with improved defenses, such as strong encryption and Cloud-based solutions – though they will help – too little is done to winkle out and extirpate the cyber bandits still roaming the virtual domain. If left out there, they will first naturally shift to searching for targets with very poor defenses: the "easy pickings." But, at the same time, they will study the well-defended spaces and, eventually, develop new means with which to launch effective attacks. And this might happen quite soon for those cyber bandits in the employ of nations with the expertise and resources to give them a big capability boost.

Something aside from defenses should be cultivated. Potentially, a decisive approach to the sharp reduction, if not the near-elimination, of cyber banditry would consist of crafting a proactive capacity for detecting malefactors as they move about in cyberspace. The goal of this would be cyber-locating them, determining their physical locations, and possibly, in some settings, arresting or extraditing them. This can be done, given that cyber bandits spend huge amounts of time searching for prime targets – often with AI "scouts" – which sooner or later makes them vulnerable to detection by skilled trackers. But who are these hunters, and how will they operate?

Tracking can be conducted in a constrained way by in-house official personnel, or, more loosely, by hiring hackers from the "outside" – all within the limits imposed by legal and ethical hurdles that delimit their allowable range of action in liberal societies. For example, attempts to "back hack" intruders tend to be curtailed once a trail leads beyond homeland borders (in terms of locations of sites employed by the hostiles). So, in addition to what can be done by national law-enforcement, military, and intelligence actors, it may prove fruitful for nations to develop covert links with top-flight hackers who remain "in the virtual wild," and perhaps even with some known to have engaged in cyber banditry themselves. They are the ones most likely to be able to detect, track, and disrupt other bandits, guide the authorities to the malefactors, or prey directly upon them.

There is historical precedent for this last notion, of using bandits to attack and drive back other bandits. In Russia, for centuries, the Cossacks ("free men," though some etymological analysis suggests the word also has a link to banditry) protected the frontiers from Tartar bandits who engaged in theft and mass kidnapping along the southern frontiers of Muscovy. In 1654, the Czar even went so far as to give Cossacks the rights to "administer the country and collect the taxes" in what is now Ukraine. This was because they had proved able to thwart the Tartars, raiding them mercilessly. As historian Bernard Pares noted of the prowess of the Cossacks, "They possessed wonderful military resource and were masters at taking cover . . . They were ready for anything."[7]

It is hard to conceive of a modern government giving administrative authority of this sort to a band of hackers – even the whitest of "white hats" – but, such enablement aside, the idea of using consummate raiders to track and attack dangerous criminals, insurgents, or terrorists is quite well worth considering. Another example of this sort of arrangement, with less official governmental cession of local rule to the protecting party, can be seen in the period of the British Raj in India. There were numerous cases, throughout the colonial period, of the use of friendly *dacoits* who served to prevent the depredations of yet other bandits. Of especial interest were the Ramosi, whose operating area during the nineteenth century was the Bombay Presidency. In return for guarding the passing caravans and settled villages in the area, the Raj granted the Ramosi both land and the right to charge a toll to all travelers.[8] While this method of compensation could not be offered to hackers today – even to trusted ones committed to service against cyber banditry – they *could* be permitted to take from those whose malign acts they were able to prevent or pre-empt. Of course, providing indirect compensation of this sort would require careful auditing, if not routine monitoring, so that the friendly hackers would be less likely to strike simply at juicy targets – whether of the guilty or the innocent.

Such an effort to operate more freely, but with at least a modicum of topsight over these virtual "hunter networks" – the term for them that I first recommended back in 2007 – has an interesting precedent in the British use of "pseudo gangs" in Kenya versus the Mau Mau in the 1950s, and thereafter in a number of other colonial settings. The basic idea is to "turn" captured militants, or to employ those who could pose convincingly as them, then set them loose to link up with the various cells and nodes of criminal, insurgent, or terrorist networks. Once they were identified and located, official forces would swoop down upon them.

The pseudo cell would remain on the prowl for others. This method was developed by the British intelligence officer Frank Kitson, who used it in Kenya, Oman, and even in Northern Ireland. In each case, sustained successes were achieved where victory had eluded the earlier, more conventional methods applied. As Kitson summed up the key challenge, "The problem of defeating insurgents consists very largely of *finding* them."[9] The same is true in terms of the highest priority for dealing with malign hackers in cyberspace: they must be found if they are to be fought. And who better to help in the finding process than other hackers, operating outside the constraints imposed by officialdom? It is a solution waiting to be applied.

Yet, to a great extent, it is a solution still awaiting adoption. Of my own efforts, undertaken with what Americans call the "interagency community," I am allowed only to say that the process has proved highly problematic. Part of this is the result of difficulties with properly vetting candidates for "pseudo teams," and the common response among officials that "We can grow our own top-flight hackers." Self-development of this sort is, to be sure, going on. But it takes time; and internally grown hackers are never going to have the same qualities and sensibilities as operators who have always been in the wild. These "wildlings" – some of whom I have come to know well personally – are drawn to the beauty and complexity of cyberspace. They treasure it; many seek to help to secure it from acts of postmodern banditry. John Carlin and Garrett Graff have described very well the ethos of the first generation of these cyber actors – which persists among some today – noting how they have "subscribed to a shared online code . . . focused on openness, the decentralization of information, and a collective responsibility to never harm data."[10] It is one of the great tragic ironies of the Information Age that master hackers, those best suited either to harm or to protect cyberspace, are embraced by authoritarians, whereas, in liberal parts of the world, they are greeted with disapproval, harassment, and prosecution.

The problem, in my view, is socio-cultural. Every new technology is accompanied by the need for a new sociology. Fresh ways of living have come with cyberspace. For example, well above a third of all American married couples began their relationships online.[11] New forms of business have arisen as well, with e-commerce rising to above $5 trillion globally – prior to the COVID-19 pandemic. This is about 6 percent of global GDP, and is greater in size than all but the American and Chinese economies, which account for roughly 40 percent of world output. And, yes, new ways of war have arisen, too – of both large-scale military and irregular types of action, including the emergence of terrorism as a form of war in its own right. Here, too, the challenge of redesigning military affairs, as catalyzed and guided by the emergence of a range of new information technologies, has remained unmet.

Understanding *Bitskrieg*: The purely military dimension of cyberwar

Conceptualizing cyberwar broadly – that is, with more than just cyberspace and social media in mind – requires thinking beyond how to protect one's own computers, data flows, and political discourse, along with information infrastructures, while being able to disrupt those of an enemy. The broader vision of cyberwar that David Ronfeldt and I originally envisioned in the early 1990s includes all of those elements, but also calls for an emphasis on understanding the role advanced information technologies can and should play in bringing forth revolutionary changes in military and security affairs. As former US Secretary of Defense Leon Panetta has put the matter, very succinctly, "cyber technology . . . represents a profoundly new way of thinking about combat."[12]

In my own work, I have developed the specific concept of deeply information-enhanced warfighting via a new military doctrine: *Bitskrieg,* the successor to the *Blitzkrieg* maneuver warfare doctrine that arose a century ago along with advances in mechanization.[13] *Bitskrieg* is a sub-set of cyberwar, but an important one that has been too long neglected.

Why has there been such neglect? And why does it persist? No doubt the reluctance of military professionals to change the ways with which they have been comfortable since their days as junior officers plays a part in the maintenance of the strategic and doctrinal *ancien régime.* In this, they are joined by the industrialists whose prosperity depends upon maintaining the steady flow of major ships, advanced aircraft, and ground-fighting vehicles that underpin the dominant existing views of sea, air, and land warfare. As to newer technologies – drones, hypersonic missiles, and such – these tools tend to be folded into the older military praxis. To be sure, there are some exceptions within the military ranks to norms of conformity to traditional thinking and methods. In the US Army, for example, Robert Leonhard strove to rethink *all* the standard principles of war around the basic concept that an information edge is best exploited by "dislocating" enemy forces through disruption of their communications, rather than by confrontational direct or indirect flank assaults.[14] Aside from Leonhard's path-blazing work on the principles of war, there is Douglas Macgregor's insightful effort to explore the implications of the technologies of our time for organizational redesign in his *Breaking the Phalanx*.[15] Beyond these studies, it is hard to find other signs of military thought that view the current era of technological advances as creating favorable conditions for transformational change.

The last links in the chain that binds so many societies and their militaries to older concepts – both in democracies and in many authoritarian states – are forged by those *out* of uniform: the politicians and civil servants, along with professors of military and security affairs and many other defense intellectuals. They tend to be very strongly influenced by the opinions of generals, admirals, and those defense lobbyists who use their "expertise advantage" to persuade civilian leaders in favor of military and industrial policy preferences. As Walter Millis described the situation in his classic *Arms and Men*, an exploration of American military and security affairs from the Revolution to the Cold War, the civilian sector's thought leaders "have often appeared too readily to accept the established military dogmas, and to have been timid in bringing their own critical powers to bear on questionable platitudes sanctified by generations of military experts."[16] He wrote those words in the 1950s, but they remain as relevant today as they were back then. In and beyond the United States.

All these factors – organizational, commercial, political, and social – play large parts in slowing, sometimes confusing, the ability to adapt to the implications of technological change. And it is the failure to adapt that lies, as Eliot Cohen and John Gooch have pointed out in their study of strategic catastrophes, at the heart of some of history's worst military disasters.[17]

Even if some type of behavior-based cyber arms control agreement is reached in the coming years, mutual restraint with regard to infrastructure attacks and cyberspace-based acts of political warfare will not likely lead to a broader peace. For, even though classic wars of conquest have become rare, "conflicts of contagion" – those driven by ethnic hatreds, differing god concepts, or simply to wrest control of central governance – will surely continue. At this writing, there are over 25 shooting wars under way around the world,[18] roughly the same number waged, on average, during the Cold War. That was a 40-year period (1949–89) when, referring to the looming shadow of nuclear weapons, the great scholar of *Realpolitik* Kenneth Waltz argued, "Mutual fear of big weapons may produce, instead of peace, a spate of smaller wars."[19]

Today, the risk of nuclear holocaust has much receded, at least psychologically, so, added to the "spate of smaller wars," there may even emerge a greater willingness to chance getting into larger, yet still non-nuclear, wars. This would be especially the case if a big conflict, say between great powers, could be waged in a less destructive manner. This is exactly where cyberwar and its attendant military doctrine of *Bitskrieg* come in, providing opportunities to conduct conflicts with small, nimble, networked units of soldiers, sailors, airmen, hackers – and their robotic comrades-in-arms.

Aside from envisioning a possible conflict between NATO and Russia in central Europe, or some coalition of nations bound together by the aim of thwarting Chinese expansionism in the South and East China Seas, there are middle-range powers with fearsome military capabilities of their own, quite able to cause great damage. Think of a possible conflict with Iran, if the regime of the mullahs persists in a goal of expanding regional influence and seeks to buttress its security by the development of nuclear weaponry. Or consider the chances of some crisis emerging on the Korean peninsula, whether growing from instability of the regime in the North or due to the unwillingness of Pyongyang to "denuclearize." If the United States and its allies insist upon the North completely eliminating its nuclear arsenal, the likelihood of armed conflict will only grow.

And even below the levels of the great and mid-level powers, there are the many failing and/or failed states, around the world, in which bloody conflicts already exact huge human tolls. Think of Syria, with nearly a million dead in that civil war – which has also seen military interventions by Russia, the United States, Israel, Turkey, and Iran. Then there is Yemen, where virtually the entire nation is subjected to daily horrors, from aerial bombardment to starvation. Libya, over the past decade, has suffered less, but only slightly so. In truth, our world is on fire – and the blaze may yet expand in coming years. To deal with this challenge, which is both strategic and humanitarian, the old ways will not do. Conventional military methods as employed in Iraq, Afghanistan, Syria, Yemen – and beyond – have all foundered. Only new ways offer hope.

So, the challenge for cyberwarriors today is to break out of the tightly constraining notions that emphasize only hacking and cybersecurity tools. These matter, and there is room for improving the defenses of information systems, as noted in earlier chapters. But the more urgent need – to reduce human suffering and lessen the destructiveness of armed conflict – cannot be met absent a rethinking of military affairs along lines that can only be fully understood by cultivating greater awareness of the new strategic and tactical implications of advanced, and swiftly advancing, information technologies.

The large, costly militaries of leading nations, steeped in Industrial-Age mantras of mass and sheer firepower – what some American strategists have called a doctrine of "shock and awe,"[20] which remains quite popular – will not easily make the leap to a brighter future. Traditional military methods have proved ineffective when applied in irregular wars, a troubling trend that, for example, has afflicted the American military from Vietnam to Afghanistan. So, too, the effectiveness of cyberwar will be greatly impaired if subordinated to conventional military thought. Thus, its military doctrinal component, *Bitskrieg,* needs to become "deeply integrated into state doctrine and military capabilities,"[21] according to one thoughtful study.

What would such "deep integration" look like? It would extend well beyond cyberspace, featuring fundamental shifts not just in technology, but in military doctrine, organization, and strategy as well. The doctrinal dimension addresses how to fight. Throughout the long history of military affairs, as David Ronfeldt and I have observed, battles tend to fall into one of four categories. The earliest engagements were those that tended toward chaos – in land battles and in sea fights – featuring *mêlées* that saw much confused intermixing of both sides' forces. The Greek phalanx in ancient times, the infantry battalions and naval lines of battle of the sixteenth century, and Napoleon's army corps were all attempts to achieve a quality of sheer *mass* in battle. Mass reached its evolutionary zenith *and* its dénouement in World War I, when modern weaponry wrought slaughter on the Western Front and, at the Battle of Jutland, indecisive carnage at sea. It would take the next generation of soldiers, sailors, and airmen to supersede mass by rekindling the third great doctrinal form: *maneuver.* To be sure, the all-cavalry Mongol armies of the thirteenth century were absolute masters of maneuver, as were Prussia's hard-marching infantry under Frederick the Great in the eighteenth century, given that he so often had to engage against far superior numbers. But it took modern mechanization to bring maneuver to the fore in a widely diffused, sustained way – in World War II and after.

The fourth distinct doctrinal form is what Ronfeldt and I have labeled *swarming*, a battle concept of simultaneous, omni-directional attack upon an opposing force. From ancient to medieval times, nomadic horse archers saw great value in this mode of fighting. The emergence of firearms and artillery put swarming very much into eclipse in favor of mass, for several centuries. But, over the past century, swarms re-emerged, most notably in the tactics of torpedo plane and dive-bomber squadrons – *kamikazes*, too – in the aircraft-carrier battles in the Pacific during World War II.

In the anti-colonial and other conflicts that erupted after 1945, swarm attacks were commonly the battle doctrine of choice for insurgents, reaching an especially high point in the Tet Offensive and other major actions of the Vietnam War. In our time, and for much time to come, swarming will prove to be the most effective doctrine for an era replete with Information-Age technologies that infuse weapons systems with great range and very high levels of accuracy. Those who would rely on the mantra of mass in such an age, or even on somewhat more supple traditional maneuvers, are destined to suffer defeat at ruinous cost. Needless to say, cyberspace-based attack doctrines already employ swarming, the distributed denial-of-service (DDoS) mode of offensive action being a prime example of simultaneous, omni-directional assault. That said, the greater challenge of *Bitskrieg* is to bring swarming to physical battlespaces.

Ronfeldt and I have always been careful to point out that these four archetypal doctrinal forms should be viewed as co-existing, often striving for salience in particular settings or periods of technological change.[22] Mongol doctrine was primarily focused on swift, long-ranging maneuver capability, but this was wedded to swarm tactics. Indeed, a favored battle doctrine of Genghis Khan was the omni-directional "Crow Swarm."[23] In the American Revolution, Nathanael Greene fused maneuver with swarm attacks, using his main army in the former role, his backwoods irregulars for the latter. And in World War I, T. E. Lawrence and his Arab insurgents swarmed long Turkish lines of communication, coordinating with Allenby's traditional maneuvers. But such happy syntheses developed less often in the years after the Great War. The fall of France in 1940 saw poor integration of massive positional (e.g., in the Maginot Line) and maneuver elements, leading to a very swift, catastrophic defeat. Later, in Vietnam, the US attempt to defeat insurgent swarms with massed, maneuverable, airmobile counter-swarms also failed – mostly due to the lack of stealth and extreme vulnerability of helicopters, of which over 4,000 were shot down during that war.[24]

But, if successful efforts to combine basic doctrinal forms have grown rarer, there are interesting examples of apparent awareness that swarming is *the* mode of battle most empowered in an era of increasing "informatization" – a term Chinese strategists use – of weapons systems. Russian advances by their Strategic Rocket Forces are very swarm-focused, this being viewed as the most likely way to overwhelm any missile defenses that the Americans and their allies might develop. China's missile forces are moving in this direction as well and, along with the Russians, seek to develop hypersonic speeds for these weapons. Both countries are also greatly enhancing the "information content" of these weapons with artificial intelligence, to give their guidance systems a greater capacity for stealth and evasive action.[25]

In naval affairs, Iran has for years been honing a swarm doctrine – called *esba,* which when pronounced sounds like the buzzing of bees[26] – intended for use in combat by its light coastal forces in attacks against larger enemy (likely American) vessels and fleets. In 2015, during Iran's "Great Prophet 9" exercise, a speedboat swarm very quickly destroyed a mock-up of a US carrier. More recently, Iran built another mock-up of an American carrier that was also defeated. As a thoughtful report of this exercise put the matter, "While Iran's naval forces are dwarfed by the U.S. Navy, its commanders practice so-called 'swarm tactics' aimed at overwhelming the U.S. carriers that pass through the strait on their way in and out of the Persian Gulf."[27]

The emerging Iranian concept of naval combat based on swarming provides an important clue to the linkages between technology, doctrine, and organization. Iran's swarm is best practiced by many small, heavily armed speedboats, and its navy has hundreds of them (NB: China's Navy has over 500 small missile and torpedo boats, too). And both Iran's and China's light coastal forces are organized into a large number of very small tactical assault groups. Beyond the modest weaponry each vessel carries, the real power of these forces is actualized when they come together in swarms that are both mobilized and coordinated via secure sensing and communications systems.

This is very much like the manner in which Fighter Command used Chain Home radars and the 1,000 Observer Corps outposts during the Battle of Britain to vector in dispersed Royal Air Force squadrons against the massed Luftwaffe attack formations. The traditional navies that Iranian and Chinese swarm forces are most likely to confront are still organized with most of their striking power located in just a handful of big warships, like the super-carriers of the US Navy. The increasing vulnerability of these ships to such swarm attacks is undeniable; and at the Naval Postgraduate School where I have worked over the past three decades, we have discussed, debated, and continued to wrangle over the best way to counter the growing threat from such swarm forces.

If swarming is the salient doctrine of this era in military and security affairs – and to all appearances, beyond naval matters, it is becoming so in both conventional and irregular land battles, as well as in the aerospace and cyberspace-based operational environments – then the key question revolves around the organizational form that optimizes the swarming doctrine. Much as the panzer divisions that concentrated armored power in just 10 percent of the German Army throughout World War II were the right organizational structures for that time, empowering *Blitzkrieg*, the question now is how to do the same for the swarming doctrine that will actualize the full potential of *Bitskrieg*. As I have argued throughout this book, the size of units of action should go down, but there should be far more units than currently comprise the "advanced" militaries of the world. And they need to be networked: i.e., interconnected with each other – not necessarily all with all, but in easily scalable "clusters," depending on operational situations – as well as with a coordinating (not necessarily *controlling*) command. To achieve this sort of capability, the particular demand that will be made of the leaders of today's major national militaries will be to ease the longstanding, governing notion of "command and control," and replace it with an openness to the idea of a form of command and *decontrol* that will allow swarm networks to thrive.

There have been some examples of this. Perhaps the best instance of the employment of an overall swarming approach, optimally energized by a distributed, networked organizational framework, can be glimpsed in the campaigns of Vo Nguyen Giap, who defeated both the French and American militaries in his time commanding field campaigns. The American military historian Russell Weigley judged Giap's accomplishments as "not unworthy of comparison" with the swarming campaign of Nathanael Greene during the Revolutionary War. This is high praise, given Weigley's convincing argument that, for over two centuries, Greene stood "alone as an American master developing a strategy of unconventional war."[28]

Swarms have not always swept all before them. German Admiral Karl Doenitz's "wolf pack" swarms against Allied convoys during World War II failed, mostly because he strove to maintain tight central control over them in their tactical actions – but was "hacked" by Alan Turing and the other "boffins" at Bletchley Park.[29] Doenitz's insistence upon retaining such control opened up this fatal vulnerability – a cautionary point for those who think traditional command systems can be sustained in the future.

And with regard to the importance of having secure data flows, in order to sustain the kind of swarming campaigns that will characterize a *Bitskrieg* military doctrine, one must add that, beyond security, there is also the critical need for *comprehension*. This applies not only in terms of the ability of the senior military leader to have "topsight" of the overall situation, but with sensitivity to the need of perhaps widely dispersed small units to be able to assess their best uses across the range of tactical scenarios – lest operations devolve into the most primitive form of combat, the chaotic *mêlée* that arises when there are little or no reliable information flows. This implies the value of crafting a concept of command that is far less focused on the conduits by which relevant information will travel, but rather more concentrated on ensuring that the right *content* is available in secure, timely fashion. Insight into how to strive for the right balance of emphasis between conduits and content was articulated long ago by John Diebold, one of the pioneers in the field of automation. Though his focus was not specifically military, in his path-blazing speech on "information opportunities" back in April 1980, he identified this critical challenge:

> As technology continues to rapidly change the structures and interfaces associated with information systems, understanding the implications of these changes requires looking not only at information systems . . . but at the *information content*.[30]

Thus, the art of military command itself may ultimately become closely entwined with the ability to perceive the relevance of, manage, and distribute content – at the right time – to the right clusters of units of action, whether on land, at sea, or in the aerospace and cyberspace domains. As to the content itself, the goal should always be to "structure" rather than simply to process data, so that it can then be refined into knowledge via discernment of patterns or prioritization based on the needs of any particular operational context. The great German philosopher of war, Carl von Clausewitz, was quite well aware of the increase in combat power that would come from such a process of refining and sharing-out of information. This was so important, he thought, that, as he put it, "Knowledge must become capability."[31]

Given that technology has advanced beyond Clausewitz's wildest dreams in the 200 years since he wrote *On War*, the whole business of trying to turn knowledge into capability has grown immeasurably in complexity. Not only in terms of the variety of weapons systems, but also in their high degree of accuracy at long ranges, a development that has fundamentally altered the structure, strategy, and tempo of military actions.

When one adds the absolutely oceanic tide of information flows driven by technological change – Clausewitz wrote well before even the emergence of the electric telegraph – the task for human cognition seems most daunting. As far back as the 1960s, thoughtful scholars and information scientists were growing very concerned about the problem of "information overload." Bertram Gross did pioneering work in defining and delineating this problem in his classic *Managing of Organizations*.[32] But it was futurist Alvin Toffler who raised broad public awareness that the technologies of the emerging Information Age were going to tax human cognitive capabilities to their outermost limits – more likely, beyond them. Hence the term "shock" in his *Future Shock*. As Toffler posed the problem of information overload, "overstimulation at the sensory level increases the distortion with which we perceive reality, cognitive overstimulation interferes with our ability to 'think.'"[33]

Toffler's warning is as true today as it was when written over half a century ago. And it is especially consequent in military and security affairs. This is why armed forces have become heavily reliant on computing and machine intelligence to support and sustain their key strategic analyses and operational assessments – and why cybersecurity is so critically important. Indeed, the shift to *Bitskrieg* can only occur if sufficient attention is given to the "bits" that, coming from cyberspace, pose the "subtle danger" that they will, as Jacquelyn Schneider has acutely observed, "slow down and confuse militaries, making it harder for them to carry out their missions."[34] She could have added that slowing and confusing the adversary's forces sharply reduce their combat power and greatly increases their vulnerability. There is simply no getting away from the point that operations in the virtual space are gaining ever greater capacity to affect the course of what goes on in the physical space.

This makes it all the more important that some form of behavior-based cyber arms control be considered and pursued. Military affairs and the conduct of wars have long been influenced by ameliorating agreements, from warring ancient desert nomads refraining from poisoning the water at oases to modern militaries and their societies choosing to ban the use of chemical and biological weapons – and cooperating broadly on this point, despite the fact that they continue to become involved in bitter, costly wars. Why shouldn't these sorts of ethical/humanitarian practices continue?

Toward a behavioral basis for cyber arms control

Compared to the challenges posed by making radical shifts in the approaches to cybersecurity and the conduct of military affairs, pursuing behavior-based arms control should have proved easy. It hasn't. Here the problem has been conceptual, with over-emphasis on "structural" approaches that rely upon counting and controlling dangerous materials and weapons. But because virtually all advanced information technology is dual use – "weaponizable" – any cyber arms control agreement has to be behavior-based, "operational," like those treaties that have succeeded in curtailing the production and use of chemical and biological weapons. Yet cyber is even more complex than those toxic technologies. For the various weapons of cyberwar *should* be allowable in military-versus-military actions in wartime. *Bitskrieg*'s rise as a dominant battle doctrine would be impossible without computer worms, viruses, and the other attack tools designed to confuse or cripple an enemy's information flows. So, going beyond the analogy with arms control for chemical and biological weapons, an idea should be drawn from the early efforts a century ago to restrict air power. In that instance, the basic notion was to refrain from targeting civilians. It failed in World War II, and for a while after. But it is an idea that has, for the most part, taken hold.

And so, when they met in 2015, Presidents Obama and Xi agreed to seek a behavior-based ban on cyber attacks against civil infrastructure. It was a step that has been allowed to wither – even fester, given rising Sino-American cyber tensions that led to closing China's consulate in Houston in the summer of 2020 – but which needs rekindling and nurturing now.

As noted in the preceding chapter, there was a great opportunity, back in the 1990s, to begin the process of cyber arms control between the United States and Russia. This chance for progress slipped away due to American mistrust of the Russians, and overconfidence in the durability of the perceived American lead in both the technological and psychological aspects of cyber operations. American recalcitrance was only reinforced by the opinion of the Department of Defense General Counsel in 1999, who produced a key report that argued: "There seems to be no particularly good reason for the United States to support negotiations for new treaty obligations . . . that are directly relevant to information operations."[35] In light of the cyber travails Americans have suffered, from individual to corporate security compromises, and on to the foreign effort to undermine the 2016 election – which persisted, but was much less successful in 2020 – not to mention the growing vulnerability of US armed forces to cyber attack, the General Counsel's words ring hollow.

However, for all this reluctance, the United States *did* participate in efforts, sponsored by the United Nations, to keep hopes alive that cyber arms control agreements might be reached. The first major UN meeting on this matter was held in 2005, but little progress was made. Yet efforts persisted, and at the second significant session in 2010 the United States was willing to join 14 other nations – including Britain, China, France, Germany, and Russia – in pursuing an agreement that would establish "norms of accepted behavior in cyber-space."[36] But, even at this hopeful moment, skeptics in Washington impeded progress, with President Obama's own "cyber czar" contending, in a dueling set of articles with me, that "There is no cyberwar."[37]

Needless to say, the past decade has given the lie to the idea that there is no cyberwar. There is now wide acceptance of the fact that a new form of cyberspace-based economic warfare has emerged, comprised both of costly, disruptive acts and of "strategic crime" consisting mostly of massive theft of intellectual property. Additionally, there is no doubt that the virtual domain provides a launching pad for political warfare campaigns against democratic nations – the United States being but one of the targets of such actions.

As to the aspect of cyberwar as a mode of infra-structure attack, the use most favored by air power and nuclear strategists who migrated into the cyber field,[38] the vulnerabilities identified are real, but few of these sorts of actions have occurred. This is likely because engaging in such strategic attacks in the absence of a larger ongoing war is simply a waste of valuable attack tools. When they are used in "peacetime" settings, there is ample opportunity to repair and recover from

disruptions, to learn more about how to defend infrastructure better, and to find out exactly who is behind
such attacks and punish malefactors in a variety of
ways.

Improvements in cyber forensics also make it more
likely that cyber criminals and political subversives will
be "back hacked" and held to account – along with
any nation-states that might provide them with support
and haven. Given the disutility of cyber attacks on
infrastructure, launched "out of the blue" in peacetime,
and growing risks of detection and retaliation for
intellectual property theft or political chicanery,
malefactors' sponsors, not just the targets, of these
forms of cyberwar have self-interested reasons for
engaging in behavior-based arms control agreements
that may bring order – perhaps a kind of cyber peace.
Even as the world's "hot wars" persist.

The cloudy future of armed conflict

The form of cyberwar that constitutes the path less
taken – that is, the potential to introduce revolutionary
changes in physical warfighting – is perhaps the most
important. This is why I have emphasized the new battle
doctrine of *Bitskrieg* as the key, *primus inter pares*,
element among all the various facets of cyberwar. It is
also the most daunting challenge to meet and master,
given the weight of military tradition and the pull of
political influence and commercial interest – across the
range of types of governance systems, from democracies
to full-on authoritarian states. In this sense, then, there
is far more than just a technology-based arms race
under way. Added to it is a "cognitive race" to parse
the full implications – organizational, doctrinal, and
strategic – of the new cyber tools, the winner of which

will make great gains in national power and global influence.

Technological advances matter in this race, as they have in earlier eras. Leading the way by creating heavily gunned, long-range sailing ships half a millennium ago, a handful of European states dominated (brutalizing much of) the world,[39] until the Industrial Revolution – which saw power diffuse, extending by the twentieth century to both the United States and Japan. Yet, when World War I erupted a decade later, strategy was largely replaced by mindless slaughter. Technical advances had created but a hecatomb.

The era of mechanization (and oil) followed – along with great advances in explosives, even prior to the emergence of atomic weaponry – further increasing and diffusing power and war-making potential. But the intense modern focus on technological innovations came with a severe decline in moral sensibilities that outstripped colonial depredations, and even the very worst of the great-power excesses in their wars of recent centuries past. The soldier-historian J. F. C. Fuller, writing in the wake of World War II, noted, especially of Hiroshima and Nagasaki, that

> as explosives have gone up, morality has gone down . . . leaders of the opposing nations bawl at each other like fish-wives . . . every kind of atrocity is applauded when committed against the enemy . . . the most significant fact is not the universality of these barbarities, but the popular gloating over them, which shows the degradation into which humanity has slumped.[40]

The world has witnessed nothing as large-scale as World War II over the past 75-plus years – but much of the ethos Fuller described remains. The "shock and awe" bombing that destroyed Iraq in 2003 was cheered by all too many. The explosives that today continue to rain down from the sky on the people of Yemen have made that very sad land the world's charnel house – yet the war drags on, given unremitting Saudi hatred of the insurgent Houthis, and unflagging Iranian support for those tribesmen.

There is a touch of veiled barbarity, too, in the fact that the nuclear peace of our time rests on a foundation of persistent threats to annihilate hundreds of millions of innocents in a great-power mutual suicide pact that would undoubtedly bring down the world social system, perhaps even the environmental basis for sustainable life on the planet. Clearly, the story of technology and military affairs is double-edged. New forms of war-making have indeed emerged, ever shifting the face of battle. But each new type of weaponry has ultimately led to cataclysm, a vastly greater ability to strike at noncombatants directly, and, most recently, to the deadliest stalemate of all, whose alternative is nuclear holocaust.

Given the foregoing, a cognitive leap is required, to help think in terms of the consequences of coming advances in military and security affairs – which will include really smart robots. And here there is hope. The various dimensions of cyberwar tend more toward the disruptive, not the destructive. Even its specifically military aspect, *Bitskrieg,* implies an emerging ability to engage with much smaller numbers, to win battles by severing or confounding enemy communications, and, by its very emphasis on being scaled down, to shore up deterrence and encourage arms control.

Yet even here there is a paradox: a revolutionary leap in military affairs might actually encourage war-making and limit the attractions of arms control. But it does seem possible that wide adoption of *Bitskrieg,* along with much smarter cybersecurity and a clear, expressed willingness to forgo attacks on civilian infrastructures via arms control, can actually work in tandem to shore up deterrence and sustain a more peaceful world. When war does break out, it can be waged, if more disruptively, at the least less destructively. As to arms control in a world where wars are still likely to occur, Thomas Schelling and Morton Halperin made the case for the value of such negotiated agreements, even when armed conflicts do arise. As they observed, arms control "involves strong elements of mutual interest in the avoidance of a war . . . *and* in curtailing the scope and violence of war in the event it occurs."[41] Thus, whether one believes in the prospect of attaining a durable peace in the Information Age – call it the *Pax Cybernetica* – or in the inevitability of continuing armed conflict, there are good reasons both to seek out and glimpse the next face of battle *and* to forge agreements that will limit the scope of disruption, physical destruction, and loss of life in conflict.

On this last point, about the human cost of war, advances in artificial intelligence may prove especially useful, as robots could come to replace many of the human soldiers, sailors, and airmen of the combat arms. An excellent existence proof of the great potential of "AI Jane" came recently in a rigorous test of the Deep Mind robot, which was pitted, in the summer of 2020, against one of the best American "Top Gun" fighter pilots in a series of dogfights. Both human and bot pilots were operating flight simulators (of the same aircraft type) and, over the course of five encounters, Deep Mind won each time – without suffering a single "hit" inflicted by the human pilot. It is a clear indication of how machine intelligence is destined to become even more widespread in, and influential to, the future of military affairs. Needless to say, the ubiquitous presence of intelligent warfighting machines creates a need both to recognize that this use of AI will not be subject to a behavior-based arms control agreement, and to realize that the ethical concerns about waging war justly become even more important when bots start doing the fighting.[42] This raises an overarching question that goes beyond the major challenges that I believe should be emphasized by senior civilian and military leaders. And it perhaps provides a deeper explanation of the failure to meet and master these challenges.

Needed: a new mindset and culture

On reflection, I have come to the belief that the failure to deal effectively with the challenges posed by the new technologies of this era can only be explained – and ultimately rectified – by developing an understanding that is broader than the notion of an opposition to change, among countries around the world, comprised of hidebound militaries, shortsighted industrialists, and parochially oriented political leaders. Such an understanding would be less focused on criticism of the flawed reasoning of decision makers and more attuned to the overarching societal inflection point that has been reached in human–machine relations. Much as the printing press sparked intellectual renewal – and the Reformation[43] – half a millennium ago, and the steam engine that launched the Industrial Revolution changed the world yet again, now the Information Age has come with a similarly powerful impact. So much so that, as the historian of technology Elting Morison described the state of affairs when he considered emerging information systems – even the creation of a virtual domain – back in the 1960s, "We have produced . . . an artificial environment of such complication that we cannot control it."[44]

In Morison's view, the failure to adapt to the implications of the latest revolutionary technological changes
results less from specific deficiencies in commercial,
governmental, and social institutions, and more from
the stickiness of culture, the rerouting of whose currents
is a major undertaking. He posed the challenge this
way: "If we are to manage the powerful system we
have created . . . we must also create a new sort of
culture that will give clear definition to what, in the new
scheme of things, our interests really are." In practical
terms, this meant not always careening about at ever
higher speed, more centralization, and massive scaling
up, but rather an approach based on a well-tempered
pace of advance, and willingness to decentralize and
"scale down." In short, Morison hoped to see a very
deliberate, sustained effort to identify and adapt to the
cultural implications of technological change that would
avoid the difficulties arising when the tempo of advance
in machinery far outstrips the conscious sensibilities
of the creators.[45] This point about the need to think in
larger cultural terms resonates especially profoundly as
we contemplate the future of automation and the rise
of intelligent machines. It is, in the view of long-time
observer of technology trends John Markoff, a central
challenge of our time.[46]

How, then, do we proceed in a time when machine
advances come fast and furious, while slower-moving
cultural perspectives impede the pace of change in
all sorts of organizations and social groupings? It
is a question that the British biologist – and Darwin
supporter – Thomas Huxley raised in the nineteenth
century when he surveyed industrial progress and
famously asked, "What are you going to do with all
these things?" For Elting Morison, who pondered an
even wider range of new "things" a century later, the
way to avoid being psychologically overwhelmed by

the sheer scale of change, and driven to cling to the reassurance of older ways, is to engage in a selective series of societal-level "experimental demonstrations."[47]

This book has outlined exactly the sort of experimentation for which Morison called. The notion of beginning a process of behavior-based cyber arms control suggests an experiment in seeing whether deterrence can be shored up and a durable peace built to secure the virtual domain upon which both society and security increasingly depend. This experiment would be strongly supported by another – one that improved cyber defenses with the ubiquitous use of the strongest encryption and widespread reliance on "the Cloud." Incentives to violate cyber arms control agreements would diminish as defenses improved by means of better encryption and data mobility.

Other cyber "experiments," which have already produced interesting results, have to do with the accrual and management of large amounts of information employed in problem solving. So-called "big data analytics" have already begun to diffuse throughout the business sector, as well as in many other domains, generating startling insights, and steady increases in productivity. An interesting example of the way in which big data analysis has been employed successfully has been in the contact-tracing efforts aimed at controlling the spread of the COVID-19 virus. In country after country – especially in East Asia, but with some glaring exceptions, as in the United States – data gathering and analysis has played a major role in curtailing outbreaks. A dramatic example of what is possible can be found in the case of the Colombian city of Medellín. By mid-June of 2020, over three months into the global pandemic, this city with a population of over 2.5 million – with another million in its immediate surroundings – had just over 700 cases, with only 10 hospitalizations. Despite high density of a population that has a very large proportion of poor, virtually all followed the strict quarantine guidelines about sheltering in place and, thanks to a cellphone app, food was delivered to the needy and infection data collected and swiftly acted upon. Information management was the key to this success.[48]

In the fight against terrorism, skillful management and diffusion of information among and between intelligence and law enforcement agencies – within and across countries – have led to detection and tracking of terror networks and disruption of a range of their plots.[49] This cooperation and coordination, often between nations with pronounced differences in other areas, has provided experimental proof of the sort that Elting Morison suggested could shift long-held mindsets. As I have always said, in briefing senior decision makers, "In an earlier era, your power was measured in terms of information you could control; now, and in the future, your strength will be gauged by the amount of information you *share.*"

While this sort of cooperation/networking in the management and use of information lies at the heart of key aspects of a broad, multi-dimensional concept of cyberwar, the experimental existence proofs have, to date, still done little to prompt wider diffusion of best practices. This is due partly to long-held habits of mind that, even at the highest levels, are hard to move. But not impossible, especially if Morison's idea of looking for experimental demonstrations is taken to heart, and evidence gleaned from them is given serious, honest consideration.

The ultimate challenge, then, is to think anew about the world and how we live, love, work, and fight in it. The problem with meeting this daunting challenge is that in most countries, on a spectrum ranging from liberal to authoritarian forms of governance, the power elites are generally older, and far less likely to understand or embrace the new socio-cultural frames of reference and behavior. Indeed, in many countries tending toward a generally older demographic, their mass publics, not just the leaders, find adjustment to the new too difficult, prompting the rise – often in anger – of retrogressive populist movements. In recent years, this sort of reaction has emerged in the United States, as well as in other countries where so-called "nationalist populist movements" have arisen. So, it is hardly a surprise that adjustment to the societal and security implications of this Information Age have thus far been very dangerously neglected. This is a neglect that will surely impose ruinous costs – in the social, commercial, and military realms – if allowed to continue.

And as dangerous as it is to fail to emphasize the military doctrine best suited to this Information Age – *Bitskrieg* – it is nearly as perilous to continue to base the approach to cybersecurity primarily on firewalls and anti-viral software. The very costly blows that hackers are inflicting on individuals, businesses, and institutions should prompt a willingness to contemplate a major shift to an approach primarily reliant upon wide use of strong encryption and Cloud computing. Yet here, despite overwhelming evidence, the impediments to change are as telling as in the military realm. There are the same habits of mind and institutional interests in this area, keeping societies and their security path-dependent on firewalls and anti-virals. There is also pressure to sustain the business sector built upon these tools – though there are signs the tight grip of leading firms is loosening, and that the approach to cybersecurity is broadening. But, in the meantime, this too limited way of approaching cybersecurity not only keeps information systems insecure – it impedes progress in diffusing the most advanced forms of communication, as exemplified by the protracted contretemps regarding China's involvement in, and possible access to, the information and system controls involved with 5G technology.[50] Emphasizing "strong crypto and the Cloud" would greatly ease the putative risks associated with adoption of the Huawei firm's 5G system – especially since Huawei has, on occasion, offered to share its source code. Taking a broader approach to cybersecurity will make it easier to enjoy boosts in speed and efficiency that 5G promises.

In sum, the main challenges outlined above, and throughout this book, speak to: (1) better securing connectivity and information – both stored and flowing – enabling great socio-economic progress; (2) embracing the major change in military and security affairs that the most cutting-edge information technologies enable – *Bitskrieg*, the new face of battle; and (3) rethinking the arms control concept so as to apply it to cyber operations, improving the prospects for controlling arms races and crises – but also to limit the damage done, particularly to civilian infrastructures, when armed conflicts do erupt.

As I look back on the several decades of my life that have been devoted to identifying better ways to pursue information security, mitigate conflict, and foster arms control, I see that little progress has been made in the direction of *any* of these challenges. Even though these issues have been around for some time – disruptive hacking, protracted, indecisive wars, and arms racing – and all are becoming more pernicious, they are still "new" in the sense that the most effective policies for dealing with them remain to be adopted. The greatest challenge of all, then, may be to recognize that current approaches to dealing with the growing threat of mass disruption will not suffice. Such recognition, if achieved, will open up opportunities for innovative advances that lead to enduring solutions, and to the betterment of society and security in an era transformed by information technologies. May it be so.

Notes

1 "Cool War" Rising

1 Carl von Clausewitz, *On War*, ed. and trans. Michael Howard and Peter Paret (Princeton University Press, 1976), p. 89.

2 Martin Libicki, *Conquest in Cyberspace* (Cambridge University Press, 2007), p. 2. See also his *What Is Information Warfare?* (Washington, DC: National Defense University Press, 1995). His "mosaic of forms" phrasing first appeared on p. 3 of the earlier study.

3 See Robert S. Mueller III, *Report on the Investigation into Russian Interference in the 2016 Presidential Election* (Washington, DC: Government Printing Office, 2019).

4 Clausewitz, *On War*, p. 84.

5 Cited in David E. Sanger and Julie Hirschfeld Davis, "Data Breach Tied to China Hit Millions," *The New York Times*, June 5, 2015.

6 See Damian Paletta, "OPM Breach Was Enormous, FBI Director Says," *The Wall Street Journal*, July 8, 2015.

7 Lily Hay Newman, "Hack Brief: 885 Million Sensitive Financial Records Exposed," *Wired*, May 24, 2019.

8 Eric Tucker, "US Researchers Warned of Theft," Associated Press, October 7, 2019.

9 See Michael McGuire, *Into the Web of Profit: Understanding the Growth of the Cybercrime Economy* (Cupertino, CA: Bromium, Inc., 2018).

10 "North Korea Targets Cryptocurrency Exchanges, Banks" (New York: United Nations Security Council), August 5, 2019.

11 This theme is explored in Florian Egloff, "Cybersecurity and the Age of Privateering," in George Perkovich and Ariel E. Levite, eds., *Understanding Cyber Conflict: 14 Analogies* (Washington, DC: Georgetown University Press, 2017), especially p. 233.

12 George Quester, *Offense and Defense in the International System* (New York: John Wiley & Sons, 1977).

13 See Thomas Rid, *Cyberwar Will Not Take Place* (Oxford University Press, 2013).

14 On cyber aspects of this conflict, see John Markoff, "Before the Gunfire, Cyberattacks," *The New York Times*, August 12, 2008. See also Ronald Asmus, *A Little War That Shook the World* (New York: St. Martin's Press, 2010).

15 Adam Meyers, "Danger Close: Fancy Bear Tracking of Ukrainian Field Artillery Units," *CrowdStrike*, December 2016, revised March 2017.

16 On the Ivano-Frankivsk infrastructure attack, and Tom Bossert's estimate of the cost of the damage done, see Andy Greenberg, "The Untold Story of NotPetya, the Most Devastating Cyberattack in History," *Wired* (August 2018).

17 The classic account of this conflict is still Hugh Thomas's *The Spanish Civil War* (New York: Harper & Brothers, Publishers, 1961).

18 For more detail, see Charles Messenger, *The Blitzkrieg Story* (New York: Charles Scribner's Sons, 1976), p. 127.

19 Karl-Heinz Frieser and J. T. Greenwood, *The Blitzkrieg Legend: The 1940 Campaign in the West* (Annapolis: Naval Institute Press, 2005), p. 10.

20 From William L. Shirer, *The Rise and Fall of the Third Reich* (New York: Simon and Schuster, 1960), pp. 701, 703.

21 This view is thoughtfully exposited in Scott Shane, *Dismantling Utopia: How Information Ended the Soviet Union* (Chicago: Ivan R. Dee, 1994).

22 Donald Coers, *John Steinbeck Goes to War: The Moon Is Down as Propaganda* (Tuscaloosa: University of Alabama Press, 2006).

23 Cited in Steve Sheinkin, *Bomb: The Race to Build – and Steal – the World's Most Dangerous Weapon* (New York: Roaring Brook Press, 2012), p. 163.

24 Cited in David E. Sanger, *Confront and Conceal: Obama's Secret Wars and Surprising Use of American Power* (New York: Crown Publishers, 2012), p. 200.

25 Nicole Perlroth, "Cyberattack on Saudi Firm Disquiets U.S.," *The New York Times*, October 24, 2012.

26 See Samuel Gibbs, "Triton: Hackers Take Out Safety Systems in Watershed Attack on Energy Plant," *The Guardian*, December 15, 2017; and Martin Giles, "Triton is the World's Most Murderous Malware – and It's Spreading," *Technology Review*, March 5, 2019.

27 Frederik Pohl, *The Cool War* (New York: Del Rey Books, 1981).

28 Joseph Nye, "Deterrence and Dissuasion in Cyberspace," *International Security*, 41, 3 (2017), p. 55.

29 Norbert Wiener, *The Human Use of Human Beings* (London: Eyre & Spottiswoode, 1954).

30 See John Arquilla and David Ronfeldt, "Cyberwar Is Coming!" *Comparative Strategy*, 12, 2 (April–June, 1993), pp. 141–65. Quotes are from pp. 141, 145. Emphasis added.

31 John Keegan, *The Second World War* (New York: Viking, 1990), p. 87.

32 *Ibid.*, p. 156.

33 Michael Carver, "Conventional Warfare in the Nuclear Age," in Peter Paret, ed., *Makers of Modern Strategy* (Princeton University Press, 1986), p. 803. On the Six-Day War, see Michael B. Oren, *Six Days of War* (Oxford University Press, 2002).

34 C. Kenneth Allard, "The Future of Command and Control: Toward a Paradigm of Information Warfare," in L. Benjamin Ederington and Michael J. Mazarr, eds., *Turning Point: The Gulf War and U.S. Military Strategy* (Boulder: Westview Press, 1995), p. 163.

35 See Roger C. Molander, Andrew S. Riddile, and Peter A. Wilson, *Strategic Information Warfare: A New Face of War* (Santa Monica: RAND, 1996). A comprehensive early study of the Pentagon's narrower conception of cyberwar, and the choice to focus on it primarily as a mode of strategic attack, can be found in Gregory Rattray, *Strategic Warfare in Cyberspace* (Cambridge, MA: The MIT Press, 2001).

36 The movie was based on Harry Bates's short story, "Farewell to the Master," published in the October 1940 issue of *Astounding Science Fiction*. The story was novelized by Arthur Tofte, *The Day the Earth Stood Still* (London: Scholastic, Inc., 1976). While the original Klaatu acted carefully and demonstratively, the aliens in the 2008 remake of the film, starring Keanu Reeves, chose to intervene more destructively, in the end denying humanity any use of electricity.

37 Robert A. Pape's *Bombing to Win: Air Power and Coercion in War* (Ithaca: Cornell University Press, 1996) is a comprehensive study of the limits of strategic aerial bombardment. See also Tami Davis Biddle, *Rhetoric and Reality in Air Warfare: The Evolution of British and American Ideas about Strategic Bombing, 1914–1945* (Princeton University Press, 2002).

38 James Adams, *The Next World War: Computers Are the Weapons and the Front Line Is Everywhere* (New York: Simon & Schuster, 1998), p. 97.

39 For insight into this perspective, see Wesley Clark, *Waging Modern War: Bosnia, Kosovo, and the Future of Combat* (New York: PublicAffairs, 2001), especially pp. 259, 342–3.

40 Ivo H. Daalder and Michael E. O'Hanlon, *Winning Ugly: NATO's War to Save Kosovo* (Washington, DC: Brookings Institution Press, 2000).

41 See John Arquilla and David Ronfeldt, "Need for High-Tech, Networked Cyberwar," *The Los Angeles Times*, June 20, 1999.

42 The most detailed account of this campaign can be found in Doug Stanton, *Horse Soldiers* (New York: Scribner, 2009).

43 See Donald H. Rumsfeld, "Transforming the Military," *Foreign Affairs* (May/June 2002).

44 John Keegan, *The Iraq War* (New York: Alfred A. Knopf, 2004), p. 145.

45 Lieutenant General Paul Van Riper USMC (Ret.) and Lieutenant Colonel F. G. Hoffman USMCR, "Pursuing the Real Revolution in Military Affairs: Exploiting Knowledge-Based Warfare," *National Security Studies Quarterly*, 4, 1 (Winter 1998), p. 12.

46 Michael Maclear, *The Ten Thousand Day War: Vietnam 1945–1975* (New York: St. Martin's Press, 1981), p. 191.

47 Victor Davis Hanson, *The Savior Generals: How Five Great Commanders Saved Wars That Were Lost – From Ancient Greece to Iraq* (London: Bloomsbury Press, 2013), p. 229. On this same point, see also Thomas E. Ricks, *The Gamble: General David Petraeus and the American Military Adventure in Iraq, 2006–2008* (New York: The Penguin Press, 2009), p. 163.

48 António Guterres, "Remarks at Web Summit," United Nations, November 8, 2018.

49 Cited in Samuel Gibbs, "Musk, Wozniak and Hawking Urge Ban on Warfare AI and Autonomous Weapons," *The Guardian*, July 28, 2015.

50 Michael Crichton, *Electronic Life: How to Think About Computers* (New York: Alfred A. Knopf, 1983), pp. 135–6.

51 For a concise overview of military applications of robotics, see John Arquilla, "Meet A.I. Joe," *Communications of the Association for Computing Machinery*, May 1, 2015.

52 Kai-Fu Lee, *AI Superpowers: China, Silicon Valley, and the New World Order* (Boston: Houghton Mifflin Harcourt, 2018), provides an excellent overview of this new competition.

53 See, for example: Ewen Montagu, *Beyond Top Secret Ultra* (New York: Coward, McCann & Geoghegan, Inc., 1978); David Kahn, *Seizing the Enigma* (Boston: Houghton Mifflin, 1991); and John Prados, *Combined Fleet Decoded* (New York: Random House, 1995).

54 Marshall   McLuhan,   *Understanding   Media: The*

Extensions of Man (New York: McGraw-Hill Book Company, 1965), p. 23.

55 *Ibid.*, p. 27.

56 On the first three of these, in Georgia, Ukraine, and Kyrgyzstan, see Lincoln A. Mitchell, *The Color Revolutions* (Philadelphia: University of Pennsylvania Press, 2012).

57 See Kevin Kelly, "We Are the Web," *Wired* (August 2005).

58 John Arquilla and David Ronfeldt, *Networks and Netwars: The Future of Terror, Crime, and Militancy* (Santa Monica: RAND, 2001).

2 Pathways to Peril

1 Richard A. Clarke and Robert K. Knake, *Cyber War: The Next Threat to National Security and What to Do about It* (New York: HarperCollins, 2010), especially p. 148.

2 From a speech at the Carnegie Endowment for International Peace, September 20, 2011.

3 Norman Cousins, *The Pathology of Power* (New York: W. W. Norton, 1987), p. 194.

4 See Nicholas Burns and Douglas Lute, *NATO at Seventy: An Alliance in Crisis* (Cambridge, MA: Belfer Center for Science and International Affairs, 2019).

5 Patrick Tucker, "NATO Getting More Aggressive in Offensive Cyber," *Defense One*, May 24, 2019.

6 See, for example, Ian Grant, "U.S. Computers Still Insecure after Spending Billions," *Computer Weekly*, March 25, 2010.

7 Cited in Craig Timberg, "Net of Insecurity: A Flaw in the Design," *The Washington Post*, May 30, 2015.

8 Fred Kaplan, *Dark Territory: The Secret History of Cyber War* (New York: Simon & Schuster, 2016), p. 8. Ware's path-blazing study is *Security and Privacy in Computer Systems* (Santa Monica: RAND, 1967), P-3544.

9 See Dorothy E. Denning and Peter J. Denning, eds., *Internet Besieged* (Boston: Addison-Wesley, 1998).

10 Steven Levy, *Crypto* (New York: Penguin Books, 2001), p. 63.

11 See Steven Levy, "Battle of the Clipper Chip," *The New York Times*, June 12, 1994.

12 Both quotes from Katarzyna Lasinska, "Encryption Policy Issues in the EU," *Global Policy Watch*, May 25, 2018. Also posted in EU Law and Regulatory Archives, www.nationalarchives.gov.uk.

13 For an excellent overview of the Snowden affair as it unfolded in 2013, see Mirren Gidda, "Edward Snowden and the NSA Files – Timeline," *The Guardian*, August 21, 2013. See also: the series of *Guardian* articles that Glenn Greenwald wrote about this matter, and his *No Place to Hide* (New York: Metropolitan Books, 2014); documentary film maker Laura Poitras's 2014 *Citizenfour*; and Edward Snowden, *Permanent Record* (New York: Metropolitan Books, 2019).

14 Cited in Amanda Holpuch, "Tim Cook Says Apple's Refusal to Unlock iPhone for FBI is a 'Civil Liberties' Issue," *The Guardian*, February 22, 2016.

15 See Ellen Nakashima, "FBI Paid Hackers One-Time Fee to Crack San Bernardino iPhone," *The Washington Post*, April 12, 2016.

16 Both quotes are from Eric Geller, "Apple Rebukes DOJ over Pensacola iPhone Encryption Battle," *Politico*, January 14, 2020.

17 Drew Harwell, "Google to Drop Pentagon AI Contract after Employee Objections to the 'Business of War,'" *The Washington Post*, June 1, 2018.

18 Cited in Ted Koppel, *Lights Out: A Cyberattack, A Nation Unprepared, Surviving the Aftermath* (New York: Crown Publishers, 2015), p. 15.

19 *Ibid.*, p. 8.

20 Israel G. Lugo and Don Parker, "Software Firewalls: Made of Straw?" *Symantec Connect*, June 7, 2005.

21 Michael Thornton, "You Can't Depend on Antivirus Software Anymore: Malware has Become too Sophisticated," *Slate*, February 16, 2017.

22 P. W. Singer and Allan Friedman, *Cybersecurity and Cyberwar: What Everyone Needs to Know* (Oxford University Press, 2014), p. 63. Emphasis added.

23 David Kahn, *The Codebreakers: The Story of Secret Writing*, revised edition (New York: Scribner, [1967] 1996), p. 84.

24 *Ibid.*, p. 412. The large number of possibilities per keystroke is calculated by raising 26 to the fourth power, as each rotor created a fresh alphabet with each input. See also Kahn's *Seizing the Enigma* (Boston: Houghton Mifflin, 1991), and, specifically about Bletchley, F. H. Hinsley and Alan Stripp, eds., *Codebreakers: The Inside Story of Bletchley Park* (Oxford University Press, 1994).

25 See Scott Aaronson, "Why Google's Quantum Supremacy Milestone Matters," *The New York Times*, October 30, 2019.

26 Emily Grumbling and Mark Horowitz, eds., *Quantum Computing: Progress and Prospects* (Washington, DC: The National Academies Press, 2019), especially p. 95.

27 Kate Conger, David Sanger, and Scott Shane, "Microsoft Wins Pentagon's $10 Billion JEDI Contract, Thwarting Amazon," *The New York Times*, October 25, 2019.

28 Conor Gearty, *Terror* (London: Faber and Faber, 1991), p. 2.

29 Paul Wilkinson, *Terrorism versus Democracy: The Liberal State Response* (London: Routledge, [2001] 2006), p. 195.

30 Richard English, *Terrorism: How to Respond* (Oxford University Press, 2009), p. 129. For an exceptionally thorough, thoughtful exposition of the whole debate about the efficacy of terrorism, see also his *Does Terrorism Work?* (Oxford University Press, 2016).

31 Walter Laqueur, "Postmodern Terrorism," *Foreign Affairs* (September/October 1996), pp. 24–36; quote from p. 35. On the less physically disruptive end of the spectrum of cyberterror, see Gabriel Weimann, *Terror on the Internet: The New Arena, the New Challenges* (Washington, DC: United States Institute of Peace Press, 2006).

32 David E. Sanger, *The Perfect Weapon: War, Sabotage, and Fear in the Cyber Age* (New York: Crown Publishers, 2018). Sanger's account speaks particularly well to the threat of "mass disruption."

33 Thomas M. Chen, *Cyberterrorism After Stuxnet* (Seattle: Didactic Press, 2015), p. 1.

34 Robert T. Marsh, *Critical Foundations: Protecting America's Infrastructure* (Washington, DC: Government Printing Office, 1997), p. 15.

35 David Tucker co-led and co-edited this study with me: *Cyberterror: Prospects and Implications* (Monterey: Center for the Study of Terrorism and Irregular Warfare, 1999). The working group – and principal authors – consisted of Air Force Major William Nelson, Army Majors Michael Iacobucci and Mark Mitchell, Marine Corps Major Rodney Choi, and Air Force Captain Greg Gagnon.

36 Cited in Gerald McKnight, *The Terrorist Mind* (New York: The Bobbs-Merrill Company, Inc., 1974), p. 24.

37 On these points, see: Robert Pape, *Dying to Win: The Strategic Logic of Suicide Terrorism* (New York: Random House, 2005); Reza Aslan, *How to Win a Cosmic War* (New York: Random House, 2009); and Jessica Stern, *The Ultimate Terrorists* (Cambridge, MA: Harvard University Press, 1999).

38 See Tim Maurer, *Cyber Mercenaries* (Cambridge University Press, 2018).

39 Krishnadev Calamur, "What is the Internet Research Agency?" *The Atlantic*, February 2018.

40 Cited in Akil N. Awan, "The Virtual Jihad," *CTC Sentinel*, 3, 5 (May 2010). This is the journal of the Combating Terrorism Center at the United States Military Academy. The quote is drawn from al-Salim's online screed, "39 Ways to Serve and Participate in Jihad," accessible at www.cia.gov by simply inputting the title.

41 William Ayers, *Fugitive Days* (London: Penguin Group, 2003), p. 261.

42 Alec Russell, "CIA Plot Led to a Huge Blast in Siberian Gas Pipeline," *The Telegraph*, February 28, 2004. The alleged plot was "outed" back then by former Secretary of the US Air Force Thomas Reed.

43 Shane Harris, "'Military-Style' Raid on California Power Station Spooks U.S.," *Foreign Policy*, December 27, 2013.

44 Both quotes from Robert Walton, "Sniper Attack on Utah Substation Highlights Grid Vulnerability," *Utility Dive*, October 13, 2016.

45 See Claire Sterling, *The Terror Network* (New York: Holt, Rinehart, and Winston, 1981); quote is from p. 13.

46 Sanche de Gramont, *The Secret War* (New York: G. P. Putnam's Sons, 1962), p. 491.

47 Brandon Valeriano, Benjamin Jensen, and Ryan Maness, *Cyber Strategy: The Evolving Character of Power and Coercion* (Oxford University Press, 2018), p. 19.

48 Jared Diamond, *Guns, Germs, and Steel: The Fates of Human Societies*, revised edition (New York: W. W. Norton & Company, 2005).

49 Eric Auchard, Jack Stubbs, and Alessandra Prentice, "New Computer Virus Spreads from Ukraine to Disrupt World," Reuters, June 27, 2017.

50 David E. Sanger, "U.S. and China Seek Arms Deal for Cyberspace," *The New York Times*, September 19, 2015.

51 Robert Axelrod and Rumen Iliev, "Timing of Cyber Conflict," *Proceedings of the National Academies of Science* (January, 2014).

52 The most thorough account of the Swartz affair is by Justin Peters, *The Idealist: Aaron Swartz and the Rise of Free Culture on the Internet* (New York: Scribner, 2016).

53 See David Kushner, "The Autistic Hacker," *IEEE Spectrum* (July 2011).

54 Maev Kennedy, "Gary McKinnon Will Face No Charges in the UK," *The Guardian*, December 14, 2012.

55 Rory Carroll, "Gary McKinnon Hacking Prosecution Called 'Ridiculous' by US Defence Expert," *The Guardian*, July 10, 2012.

56 Christa Case Bryant, "Estonia's Cyber Warriors," *The Christian Science Monitor*, February 10, 2020.

3 The Next Face of Battle

1 Bob Woodward, *Bush at War* (New York: Simon & Schuster, 2002), p. 247.

2 For a detailed account of the campaign, see Doug Stanton, *Horse Soldiers* (New York: Scribner, 2009).

3 The names used in this vignette are aliases, given the need to protect the identities of special operations forces. But I know all the principals personally, and pieced the story together from their separate accounts.

4 For more detail, see C. H. Briscoe, R. L. Kiper, J. A. Schroder, and K. I. Sepp, *Weapon of Choice: ARSOF in Afghanistan* (Ft. Leavenworth, KS: Combat Studies Press, 2003).

5 Donald Rumseld, "Transforming the Military," *Foreign Affairs* (May/June 2002).

6 John Arquilla, *Worst Enemy: The Reluctant Transformation of the American Military* (Chicago: Ivan R. Dee, 2008), p. 8.

7 See Robert V. Remini, *The Battle of New Orleans* (New York: Viking, 1999).

8 Lowell Thomas, *Raiders of the Deep* (New York: Doubleday, Doran & Company, Inc., 1928), pp. 10–28, provides a firsthand report of this action by the watch officer of the *U-9*.

9 Jeremy Black, *Tools of War* (London: Quercus Publishing plc, 2007), p. 102.

10 J. B. Bury, *History of the Eastern Roman Empire* (London: Cambridge University Press, 1912), p. 247.

11 Cyril Falls, *The Great War, 1914–1918* (New York: G. P. Putnam's Sons, 1959), p. 152.

12 See Barbara W. Tuchman, *The Zimmermann Telegram* (New York: Macmillan, 1966); and Thomas Boghart, *The Zimmermann Telegram: Intelligence, Diplomacy, and America's Entry into World War I* (Annapolis: Naval Institute Press, 2012), which benefits from freshly declassified technical details unavailable to Tuchman six decades ago.

13 Robert Morris Page, *The Origin of Radar* (New York: Doubleday & Company, Inc., 1962), pp. 176–7.

14 From Clay Blair, *Silent Victory* (New York: J. B. Lippincott Company, 1975), p. 44.

15 The doctrine was introduced in Pamphlet 525-5, "The AirLand Battle and Corps 86" (Ft. Leavenworth, KS: Training and Doctrine Command, 1981).

16 Thomas Rona, "Weapon Systems and Information War," Study ADB971302 (Washington, DC: Office of the Secretary of Defense, 1976).

17 The 1980s debate is well presented in David Bellin and Gary D. Chapman, eds., *Computers in Battle: Will They Work?* (New York: Harcourt Brace Jovanovich, 1987).

18 See, especially, L. Benjamin Ederington and Michael J. Mazarr, eds., *Turning Point: The Gulf War and U.S. Military Strategy* (Boulder: Westview Press, 1995). The chapter by Colonel Kenneth Allard, "The First Information War," speaks particularly to the outcome – swift, decisive victory for the Allies at very low cost – as being primarily a function of the information advantage enjoyed over the Iraqis.

19 Quoted in Thomas Gibbons-Neff, "Documents Reveal U.S. Officials Misled Public on War in Afghanistan," *The New York Times*, December 9, 2019.

20 On the importance of drill as a way to "embed information" in militaries, see William McNeill, *The Pursuit of Power* (University of Chicago Press, 1982), and his *Keeping Together in Time: Dance and Drill in Human History* (New York: American Council of Learned Societies, 2008).

21 P. W. Singer, *Wired for War: The Robotics Revolution and Conflict in the 21st Century* (New York: Penguin, 2009), p. 234.

22 Manuel De Landa, *War in the Age of Intelligent Machines* (Cambridge, MA: The MIT Press, 1991), p. 46.

23 John Ringo and Travis Taylor, *Von Neumann's War* (New York: Baen Books, 2006). The title reference is to John von Neumann, one of the pioneers of modern computing.

24 James F. Dunnigan, *Digital Soldiers: The Evolution of High-Tech Weaponry and Tomorrow's Brave New Battlefield* (New York: St. Martin's Press, 1996), see especially pp. 77, 79, 192.

25 Brian Nichiporuk and Carl Builder, *Information Technologies and the Future of Land Warfare* (Santa Monica: RAND, 1995), p. 53.

26 De Landa, *War in the Age of Intelligent Machines*, p. 45.

27 John Arquilla and David Ronfeldt, *Swarming and the Future of Conflict* (Santa Monica: RAND, 2000).

28 The seminal works of these three admirals are: Arthur Cebrowski and John Garstka, "Network-Centric Warfare," *Proceedings of the U.S. Naval Institute* (January 1998); Thomas Rowden, "Distributed Lethality," also in *Proceedings* (January 2015); and John Richardson, *A Design for Maintaining Maritime Superiority, 2.0* (December 2018), http://media.defense. gov > May > DESIGN – 2.0.PDF.

29 See such a reminder in Arquilla and Ronfeldt, "Swarming: The Next Face of Battle," *Aviation Week & Space Technology*, September 29, 2003.

30 David Kahn, *Seizing the Enigma* (Boston: Houghton Mifflin, 1991).

31 Vice Admiral R. R. Monroe (USN, ret.), "Short-circuiting the Electromagnetic Threat," *The Washington Times*, May 21, 2018.

32 See: David Hamblin, "Pentagon Wants Cyborg Implant to Make Soldiers Tougher," *Forbes*, June 5, 2020; and David Relman and Julie Pavlin, eds., *An Assessment of Illness in U.S. Government Employees and Their Families in Overseas Embassies* (Washington, DC: National Academies Press, 2020).

33 Cited in Frank Barnaby, *The Automated Battlefield* (New York: The Free Press, 1985), p. 1. Similar sentiments are expressed by Admiral Bill Owens, former Vice Chairman of the Joint Chiefs of Staff, throughout his *Lifting the Fog of War* (New York: Farrar, Straus & Giroux, 2000), in which he outlines his vision of a "system of systems."

34 Olivia Solon, "Man 1, Machine 1: Landmark Debate Between AI and Humans Ends in Draw," *The Guardian*, June 18, 2018.

35 Chris Bernhardt, *Turing's Vision: The Birth of Computer Science* (Cambridge, MA: The MIT Press, 2016), provides an account of this early effort to develop machine intelligence.

36 The "outpost and outreach" concept of operations is

analyzed in detail in Arquilla, *Worst Enemy*. See especially pp. 216–18.

37 The most balanced assessment of the debate about whether the addition of some troops mattered more than the radical change in the concept of operations is Thomas E. Ricks, *The Gamble: General David Petraeus and the American Military Adventure in Iraq, 2006–2008* (New York: The Penguin Press, 2009). My own argument, that the small number of new troops mattered far less than the new approach taken, can be found in my article, "The New Rules of War," *Foreign Policy* (April, 2011).

38 See Peter J. Denning and Matti Tedre, *Computational Thinking* (Cambridge, MA: The MIT Press, 2019).

39 Full schematic details of our design, and how our strategic insights were derived, can be found in Paul Davis and John Arquilla, *Deterring or Coercing Opponents in Crisis: Lessons from the War with Saddam Hussein* (Santa Monica: RAND, 1991).

40 See Megan Garber, "Funerals for Fallen Robots," *The Atlantic* (September, 2013), and Jim Edwards, "Some Soldiers Are So Attached to Their Battle Robots They Hold Funerals for Them When They 'Die,'" *Business Insider*, September 18, 2013.

41 Julie Carpenter, *Culture and Human–Robot Interaction in Militarized Spaces: A War Story* (London: Routledge, 2016).

42 See Kate Devlin, *Turned On: Science, Sex, and Robots* (Oxford: Bloomsbury, 2016).

43 For more details, see Michael Roberts, *The Military Revolution* (Oxford University Press, 1956) and his *Essays in Swedish History* (London: Weidenfeld and Nicolson, 1967). Another important study in this field is Geoffrey Parker's *The Military Revolution: Military Innovation and the Rise of the West, 1500–1800* (Cambridge University Press, 1988).

44 Michael Howard, "Men Against Fire: The Doctrine of the Offensive in 1914," in his *Lessons of History* (New Haven: Yale University Press, 1991), pp. 97–112.

45 Rumsfeld, "Transforming the Military," p. 28.

46 Colin McInnes, "Technology and Modern Warfare," in John Baylis and N. J. Rengger, eds., *Dilemmas of World Politics* (Oxford: Clarendon Press, 1992), p. 148.

47 On Russian thinking, see in particular Oscar Jonsson's thorough, thoughtful *Russian Understanding of War: Blurring the Lines Between War and Peace* (Washington, DC: Georgetown University Press, 2019). For insights into the Chinese understanding of conflict in the Information Age, see: Jeffrey Engstrom, *Systems Confrontation and System Destruction Warfare: How the People's Liberation Army Seeks to Wage Modern Warfare* (Santa Monica: RAND, 2018); and Michael Pillsbury's path-blazing anthology of translated military studies, *Chinese Views of Future Warfare* (Washington, DC: National Defense University Press, 1997).

48 Regarding the last point about networks, we developed this idea – a latter-day version of the older notion that "it takes a tank to fight a tank" – in our *Advent of Netwar* (Santa Monica: RAND, 1996). See, especially, pp. 81–2.

49 Barbara W. Tuchman, *The Guns of August* (New York: Macmillan, 1962). On this general theme, see also: George Quester, *Offense and Defense in the International System* (New York: John Wiley & Sons, 1977); and Jack Snyder, *The Ideology of the Offensive: Military Decision Making and the Disasters of 1914* (Ithaca: Cornell University Press, 1984).

50 The seminal Chinese article on remote warfare is by Shen Zhongchang, Zhang Haiyin, and Zhou Xinsheng, "21st Century Naval Warfare," in *China Military Science* (Spring 1995). Pillsbury's thoughts on this concept appear in his *Chinese Views of Future Warfare*, especially pp. xxxvii–xxxviii.

51 Erik Gartzke, "Blood and Robots: How Remotely Piloted Vehicles and Related Technologies Affect the Politics of Violence," *Journal of Strategic Studies* (October, 2019).

52 The classic modern work on "just war theory" is Michael Walzer, *Just and Unjust Wars: A Moral Argument with Historical Illustrations,* 5th edition (New York: Basic Books, [1977] 2015).

53 General Rupert Smith, *The Utility of Force: The Art of War in the Modern World* (New York: Alfred A. Knopf, 2007). An even earlier critique of war as a "usable option" can be found in Evan Luard, *The Blunted Sword: The Erosion of Military Power in Modern World Politics* (London: I. B. Tauris, 1988).

54 General Maxwell D. Taylor, *The Uncertain Trumpet* (New York: Harper & Brothers, Publishers, 1959), p. 6.

55 Julian Borger, "Trump Team Drawing Up Fresh Plan to Bolster U.S. Nuclear Arsenal," *The Guardian*, October 29, 2017.

4   (Arms) Ctrl+Alt+Esc

1 He also wrote, with Jim Newton, one of the most trenchant accounts of a life in public service, *Worthy Fights: A Memoir of Leadership in War and Peace* (New York: Penguin Press, 2014).

2 Remarks of Secretary Leon Panetta to the Business Executives for National Security, October 11, 2012.

3 James Lewis, "The Key to Keeping Cyberspace Safe? An International Accord," *The Washington Post*, October 7, 2014.

4 Martin Giles, "We Need a Cyber Arms Control Treaty to Keep Hospitals and Power Grids Safe from Hackers," *MIT Technology Review*, October 1, 2018.

5 See Robert Litwak and Meg King, *Arms Control in Cyberspace?* (Washington, DC: The Wilson Center, 2015), and Benoît Morel, "Could the United States Benefit from Cyber Arms Control Agreements?" in Phil Williams and Dighton Fiddner, eds., *Cyberspace: Malevolent Actors, Criminal Opportunities, and Strategic Competition* (Carlisle, PA: Strategic Studies Institute, 2016).

6 Dorothy Denning, "Obstacles and Options for Cyber Arms Control," in *Proceedings of the Conference on Arms Control in Cyberspace* (Berlin: Heinrich Böll Foundation, 2001), p. 3.

7 Erica D. Borghard and Shawn Lonergan, "Why Are There No Cyber Arms Control Agreements?" Council on Foreign Relations, January 16, 2018.

8 Joseph S. Nye, Jr., "The World Needs New Norms on Cyberwarfare," *The Washington Post*, October 1, 2015.

9 Martin Chulov and Helen Pidd, "Curveball: How US Was Duped by Iraqi Fantasist Looking to Topple Saddam," *The Guardian*, February 15, 2011.

10 The White House: Fact Sheet, "President Xi Jinping's Visit to the United States," September 25, 2015.

11 David Sanger, Nicole Perlroth, and Eric Schmitt, "Scope of Russian Hack Becomes Clear: Multiple U.S. Agencies Were Hit," *The New York Times*, December 14, 2020.

12 Key early studies on this theme are in Janos Radvanyi, ed., *Psychological Operations and Political Warfare in Long-term Strategic Planning* (New York: Praeger, 1990).

13 See Warwick Ashford, "US Joins UN Cyber Arms Control Collaboration," *Computer Weekly*, July 20, 2010.

14 All quotes from John Markoff, "U.S. and Russia Differ on a Treaty for Cyberspace," *The New York Times*, June 27, 2009.

15 The episode aired April 24, 2003. It is no longer available for viewing online.

16 A comprehensive overview of the varied early efforts to control the spread of weapons of mass destruction can be found in Coit Blacker and Gloria Duffy, eds., *International Arms Control: Issues and Agreements*, 2nd edition (Stanford University Press, 1984). The classic argument for managing, rather than trying to eliminate, weapons of mass destruction is Hedley Bull's *Control of the Arms Race* (New York: Praeger, 1961).

17 From his speech of November 10, 1932, in the House of Commons (*Parliamentary Debates*, Col. 638).

18 George Quester, *Deterrence Before Hiroshima* (New York: John Wiley, 1966), p. 100.

19 *Documents on Nazi Conspiracy and Aggression* (Washington, DC: Government Printing Office, 1946), Vol. III, p. 388.

20 See Rolland Chaput, *Disarmament in British Foreign Policy* (London: George Allen and Unwin, 1935), p. 344.

21 Quester, *Deterrence Before Hiroshima*, p. 106.
22 Max Hastings, *The Korean War* (New York: Simon & Schuster, 1987), p. 268.
23 Robert A. Pape, *Bombing to Win: Air Power and Coercion in War* (Ithaca: Cornell University Press, 1996).
24 Stanford Arms Control Group, J. H. Barton and L. D Weiler, eds., *International Arms Control: Issues and Agreements* (Stanford University Press, 1976), p. 202.
25 Winston S. Churchill, *The Second World War*, Vol. I, *The Gathering Storm* (Boston: Houghton Mifflin Company, 1948), p. 246.
26 A good account of the situation at the time is by Luke Harding, "What We Know about Russia's Interference in the US Election," *The Guardian*, December 16, 2016. The most recent analysis of the US government investigation into Russian political warfare led by Robert Mueller can be found in Andrew Weissman, *Where Law Ends: Inside the Mueller Investigation* (New York: Random House, 2020).
27 Thomas C. Schelling and Morton H. Halperin, *Strategy and Arms Control* (New York: The Twentieth Century Fund, 1961), p. 1.
28 Quotes from Alfred Thayer Mahan, *Armaments and Arbitration* (New York: Harper & Brothers Publishers, 1912), pp. 36–7. Emphasis added.
29 See Robert K. Massie, *Dreadnought: Britain, Germany, and the Coming of the Great War* (New York: Random House, 1991), pp. 830–2, 848–9.
30 Cited in E. L. Woodward, *Great Britain and the German Navy* (Oxford University Press, 1935), p. 418.
31 A. A. Hoehling, *The Great War at Sea: A History of Naval Action, 1914–1918* (New York: Thomas Y. Crowell, 1965), p. 188.
32 T. C. Schelling, *Arms and Influence* (New Haven: Yale University Press, 1966), p. 190.
33 Richard A. Clarke and Robert K. Knake, *Cyber War: The Next Threat to National Security and What to Do about It* (New York: HarperCollins, 2010), especially their nation-by-nation assessment on p. 148.

34 General Curtis E. LeMay and Major General Dale O. Smith, *America Is in Danger* (New York: Funk & Wagnalls, 1968), p. 44.

35 James Canan, *War in Space* (New York: Harper & Row, Publishers, 1982), p. 20.

36 See: Helen Caldicott, *War in Heaven* (New York: The New Press, 2007); Joan Johnson-Freese, *Space Warfare in the 21st Century: Arming the Heavens* (London: Routledge, 2016); and Neil deGrasse Tyson, *Accessory to War: The Unspoken Alliance Between Astrophysics and the Military* (New York: W. W. Norton & Company, 2018).

37 Quoted items from Canan, *War in Space*, pp. 19–21.

38 Cited from *Presidential Decision Memorandum 37*, May 13, 1978.

39 At this writing (2020), 109 nations have signed and ratified the Outer Space Treaty. Nearly two dozen more have signed but not yet completed the ratification process.

40 Robert Axelrod and Robert O. Keohane, "Achieving Cooperation Under Anarchy: Strategies and Institutions," in David A. Baldwin, ed., *Neorealism and Neoliberalism* (New York: Columbia University Press, 1993), p. 110.

41 Albert Legault, "The Missile Technology Control Regime," in David Dewitt, David Haglund, and John Kirton, eds., *Building a New Global Order* (Oxford University Press, 1993), p. 362.

42 Kristina Lindborg, "Hypersonic Missiles May Be Unstoppable. Is Society Ready?" *The Christian Science Monitor*, May 18, 2020.

43 For an excellent overview of this exercise, see Sydney J. Freedberg, Jr., "AI & Robots Crush Foes in Army Wargame," *Breaking Defense*, December 19, 2019.

44 John Arquilla, "Can Information Warfare Ever Be Just?" *Ethics and Information Technology*, 1, 3 (1999), pp. 203–12. Reprinted in Joel Rudinow and Anthony Graybosch, eds., *Ethics and Values in the Information Age* (London: Wadsworth, 2002).

5   **Through a Screen Darkly**

1 Steven Levy, *Crypto* (New York: Penguin Books, 2001).

2 Everett M. Rogers, *Diffusion of Innovations*, 5th edition (New York: The Free Press, [1962] 2003).

3 The 1893 paper is among a collection of writings included in Frederick Jackson Turner, *The Frontier in American History* (New York: Holt, Rinehart and Winston, [1920] 1948), quotes from pp. 3–4.

4 S. L. A. Marshall, *Crimsoned Prairie: The Indian Wars* (New York: Scribner, 1972).

5 On the types of brigands, see Eric Hobsbawm, *Bandits,* revised edition (Boston: Little, Brown [1969] 2000), especially pp. 19–25.

6 *Ibid.*, pp. 16–17 for both quotes.

7 See Bernard Pares, *A History of Russia*, definitive edition (New York: Alfred A. Knopf, [1926] 1966). Quotes from pp. 121, 176–7.

8 See R. V. Russell, *The Tribes and Castes of the Central Provinces of India*, Vol. III (London: Macmillan, 1916), pp. 237–9, 474.

9 Frank Kitson, *Low Intensity Operations* (London: Faber, 1971), p. 65. Emphasis added.

10 J. P. Carlin and G. M. Graff, *Dawn of the Code War: America's Battle Against Russia, China, and the Rising Global Cyber Threat* (New York: PublicAffairs, 2018), p. 81.

11 According to surveys done in 2013, and more recently, by the National Academy of Sciences and the Pew Research Center.

12 Leon Panetta, with Jim Newton, *Worthy Fights: A Memoir of Leadership in War and Peace* (New York: Penguin Press, 2014), p. 432.

13 See John Arquilla, "From Blitzkrieg to Bitskrieg: The Military Encounter with Computers," *Communications of the Association for Computing Machinery,* 54, 10 (October, 2011), pp. 58–65.

14 See Robert R. Leonhard, *The Principles of War for the Information Age* (Novato, CA: Presidio Press, 2000).

15 Douglas A. Macgregor, *Breaking the Phalanx: A New*

Design for Landpower in the 21st Century (New York: Praeger, 1997).

16 Walter Millis, *Arms and Men: A Study in American Military History* (New York: G. P. Putnam's Sons, 1956), p. 6.

17 Eliot A. Cohen and John Gooch, *Military Misfortunes: The Anatomy of Failure in War* (New York: The Free Press, 1990).

18 According to the Conflict Data Tracker of the Council on Foreign Relations, www.cfr.org.

19 Kenneth N. Waltz, *Man, the State, and War* (New York: Columbia University Press, 1959), p. 236.

20 See Harlan K. Ullman, James P. Wade, and L. A. Edney, *Shock and Awe: Achieving Rapid Dominance* (Washington, DC: National Defense University Press, 1996).

21 Brian M. Mazanec, *The Evolution of Cyber War: International Norms for Emerging-Technology Weapons* (Lincoln: University of Nebraska Press, 2015), p. 4.

22 The preceding paragraphs – indeed, this whole discussion of swarming – are informed by our early study of the subject. See John Arquilla and David Ronfeldt, *Swarming and the Future of Conflict* (Santa Monica: RAND, 2000).

23 Jack Weatherford, *Genghis Khan and the Making of the Modern World* (New York: Crown Publishers, 2004), p. 94.

24 Michael Maclear, *The Ten Thousand Day War: Vietnam 1945–1975* (New York: St. Martin's, 1981), p. 205.

25 These developments are examined in Lindborg, "Hypersonic Missiles May Be Unstoppable."

26 I learned this term from a former Iranian naval officer who served in these forces.

27 See: Jon Gambrell, "Amid US Tension, Iran Builds Fake Aircraft Carrier to Attack," Associated Press, June 10, 2020; and his update, "Iran Missiles Target Fake Carrier, US Bases on Alert," Associated Press, July 29, 2020.

28 The first quote comes from Russell F. Weigley, "American Strategy from Its Beginnings through the First World War," in Peter Paret, ed., *Makers of Modern Strategy*

(Princeton University Press, 1986), p. 409. The second is from his *American Way of War* (New York: Macmillan Publishing Co., Inc., 1973), p. 35. For a detailed study of Giap's concepts, see Cecil B. Currey, *Victory at Any Cost: The Genius of Viet Nam's Gen. Vo Nguyen Giap* (London: Brassey's, 1999).

29 See David Kahn, *Seizing the Enigma* (Boston: Houghton Mifflin, 1991).

30 Cited in John Diebold, *Managing Information: The Challenge and the Opportunity* (New York: American Management Association, 1985), pp. 99–100. Emphasis added.

31 Carl von Clausewitz, *On War*, ed. and trans. Michael Howard and Peter Paret (Princeton University Press, 1976), p. 147.

32 Bertram Gross, *The Managing of Organizations* (Glencoe: The Free Press, 1964).

33 Alvin Toffler, *Future Shock* (New York: Random House, 1970), p. 301.

34 Jacquelyn Schneider, "Who's Afraid of Cyberwar?" *Hoover Digest*, 2 (Spring 2020), p. 102.

35 Department of Defense General Counsel, "An Assessment of International Legal Issues in Influence Operations" (May, 1999), p. 47.

36 Warwick Ashford, "US Joins UN Cyber Arms Control Collaboration," *Computer Weekly*, July 20, 2010.

37 Howard Schmidt, "Defending Cyberspace: The View from Washington," p. 49. My response to this was "The Computer Mouse that Roared: Cyberwar in the Twenty-first Century." Both articles appeared in *The Brown Journal of World Affairs*, 18, 1 (Fall/Winter, 2011).

38 Roger C. Molander, Andrew S. Riddile, and Peter A. Wilson, *Strategic Information Warfare: A New Face of War* (Santa Monica: RAND, 1996). Another study of cyberwar as primarily a mode of strategic attack can be found in Gregory Rattray, *Strategic Warfare in Cyberspace* (Cambridge, MA: The MIT Press, 2001).

39 See Carlo Cipolla, *Guns, Sails, and Empires: Technological Innovation and the Early Phases of European Expansion*

(New York: Random House, 1965). Later on came Jared Diamond's *Guns, Germs, and Steel: The Fates of Human Societies*, revised edition (New York: W. W. Norton & Company, 2005).

40 J. F. C. Fuller, *Armament and History* (New York: Charles Scribner, 1945), p. 176.

41 Thomas C. Schelling and Morton H. Halperin, *Strategy and Arms Control* (New York: The Twentieth Century Fund, 1961), p. 1. Emphasis added.

42 For both a discussion of the aerial dogfights and the ethical implications of the AI's victory, see Will Knight, "A Dogfight Renews Concerns about AI's Lethal Potential," *Wired*, August 25, 2020.

43 See, for example, Elizabeth L. Eisenstein, *The Printing Press as an Agent of Change* (Cambridge University Press, 1980).

44 Elting E. Morison, *Men, Machines, and Modern Times* (Cambridge, MA: The MIT Press, 1966), p. 209.

45 *Ibid.*, for the quote and summary of Morison's subsequent discussion from p. 214.

46 See John Markoff, *Machines of Loving Grace: The Quest for Common Ground between Humans and Robots* (New York: HarperCollins/Ecco, 2015).

47 Morison, *Men, Machines, and Modern Times*, p. 220.

48 For an excellent account of this case, see Christine Armario, "Colombia's Medellín Emerges as Surprise COVID-19 Pioneer," Associated Press, June 14, 2020.

49 Information about these groups and thwarted plots remains largely classified. But a number of them are mentioned in Eric Schmitt and Thom Shanker, *Counterstrike* (New York: Henry Holt and Company, 2011). See ch. 7, "The New Network Warfare."

50 On this point, see Dan Sabbagh, "Cyber Security Review May Spell End for Huawei 5G Deal," *The Guardian*, May 24, 2020.

Further Reading

Beyond the books, articles, and official reports cited in the preceding chapters, I have benefited from a wide range of other readings. The cyber-related area of inquiry is quite broad, and features a surfeit of thoughtful studies. What follows, therefore, is but one slice of a very large literature. My slice.

The reader will have by now observed how much use I make of analogies. This is in part because, for all their limitations, somewhat-like things or situations, when pointed out, improve my understanding; but also because such comparisons resonate with many of the senior military leaders with whom I interact. The first systematic effort to identify analogies that could better our understanding of cyber operations was undertaken at the request of General Keith Alexander when he was the head of both the US National Security Agency and the Cyber Command. The result was a 2014 government report, *Cyber Analogies*, drawing upon experts from a range of different academic disciplines – computer science, economics, history, philosophy, politics, and psychology – that Emily Goldman and I co-edited. This effort was warmly received; and General Alexander's successor, Admiral Mike Rogers, asked for even more of this kind of thinking. What followed was a major project led by George Perkovich and Ariel E. Levite, scholars at the Carnegie Endowment for International Peace, whose co-edited volume *Understanding Cyber Conflict: 14 Analogies* (Georgetown University Press, 2017) brought together an even broader grouping of scholars.

In some respects, the effort to find ways to apply the concept of deterrence for purposes of improving the overall security of cyberspace is another analogical approach. Among the recent influential studies in this issue area, both also published in 2017, are Scott Jasper's *Strategic Cyber Deterrence* (Rowman & Littlefield) and Robert Mandel's *Optimizing Cyberdeterrence* (Georgetown University Press again).

With regard to more specifically technical approaches to protecting against hacks to one's own system, Richard Clarke and Robert Knake have followed up their 2010 *Cyber War* with a thoughtful update: *The Fifth Domain: Defending Our Country, Our Companies and Ourselves in the Age of Cyber Threats* (Penguin, 2019). As to threats from governmental Big Brothers' (and commercial Little Brothers') efforts to access large amounts of personal data about all of us, Bruce Schneier's *Data and Goliath: The Hidden Battles to Collect Your Data and Control Your World* (W. W. Norton, 2015) remains a revelation. Readers will also benefit from any of Schneier's dozen other books on how to protect oneself and one's data in cyberspace.

Given the apparent return of an era of great-power competition, as evinced by the rise of China and the return of Russia to the global stage, there have been several studies that examine how Beijing and Moscow have entered the cyber arena. These include: Dennis Poindexter, *The Chinese Information War: Espionage, Cyberwar, Communications Control and*

Related Threats to United States Interests (McFarland, 2013); Dean Cheng, *Cyber Dragon: Inside China's Information Warfare and Cyber Operations* (Praeger, 2016); Kathleen Hall Jamieson, *Cyberwar: How Russian Hackers and Trolls Helped Elect a President* (Oxford University Press, 2018); Andy Greenberg, *Sandworm: A New Era of Cyberwar and the Hunt for the Kremlin's Most Dangerous Hackers* (Doubleday, 2019); and Scott Jasper, *Russian Cyber Operations* (Georgetown University Press, 2020).

There are also some penetrating analyses of how various aspects of cyberwar affect global power politics and arms racing more broadly. Ben Buchanan has provided two: *The Cybersecurity Dilemma: Hacking, Trust and Fear between Nations* (Oxford University Press, 2017); and *The Hacker and the State: Cyber Attacks and the New Normal of Geopolitics* (Harvard University Press, 2020). On the dynamics of the emerging competition to develop cyber armaments, Nicole Perlroth's *This Is How They Tell Me the World Ends: The Cyber Weapons Arms Race* (Bloomsbury, 2020) is luminous.

Damien Van Puyvelde and Aaron Brantly, *Cybersecurity: Politics, Governance and Conflict in Cyberspace* (Polity, 2019) tie together statecraft, technology, and strategy in an incisive way. The manner in which defense firms are evolving to meet the needs of information-gathering, online war and other cyber-related demands is examined in Shane Harris, *@War: The Rise of the Military–Internet Complex* (Houghton Mifflin Harcourt, 2014). Broad explorations of the future of warfare in the Cyber Age include: David Kilcullen, *The Dragons and the Snakes: How the Rest Learned to Fight the West* (Oxford University Press, 2020); and Major General Robert Latiff, *Future War: Preparing for the New Global Battlefield* (Knopf,

2017) – the latter study reflects especial sensitivity to the moral/ethical implications of the new types of weapons systems and their contemplated uses. Though it is very focused on the United States, Christian Brose's *Kill Chain: Defending America in the Future of High-Tech Warfare* (Hachette, 2020) offers a wide-ranging analysis of the manner in which technological advances are likely to require major changes in military strategy and policy. Preceding Brose by a decade, Janine Davidson examined American defense in the Information Age from an organizational/institutional perspective in her excellent *Lifting the Fog of Peace: How Americans Learned to Fight Modern War* (University of Michigan Press, 2010).

Then there is the matter of robots. In terms of contemporary views of how they will affect the future of military and security affairs, Paul Scharre's *Army of None: Autonomous Weapons and the Future of War* (W. W. Norton, 2018) is thorough, thoughtful, even a bit chilling. And when it comes to the fictional approach to explaining the role robots will play in conflict – in this case, in the context of cyberterror – P. W. Singer and August Cole have nailed it with *Burn-in: A Novel of the Real Robotic Revolution* (Houghton Mifflin Harcourt, 2020). This brings to mind older works of related fiction that should be given fresh looks, from Karel Čapek's dystopian play, *R.U.R.*, the first musing about a robot rebellion ([Doubleday, 1922] Penguin, 2004) to Isaac Asimov's more benign, interlinked short stories, collected as *I, Robot* (Fawcett, 1950). A non-anthropomorphic, self-aware AI is featured in Robert Heinlein's *The Moon Is a Harsh Mistress* (Gollancz, [1966] 2008), a story in which the robot develops a guerrilla strategy to help lunar colonists he befriends win freedom from Earth's rule. Lest these works be dismissed, I hasten to add that many of the issues they first raised continue to resonate. One can see how they do in the influential article co-authored by Henry Kissinger, Eric Schmidt, and Daniel Huttenlocher, "The Metamorphosis" (*The Atlantic* [August, 2019]), which predicts AI will likely have "transformative" effects upon society. No doubt it will upon issues of war and peace as well.

Social media may have transformative effects, too – for good or ill. In *The Net Delusion: The Dark Side of Internet Freedom* (PublicAffairs, 2011), Evgeny Morozov makes a convincing case that connectivity can be used just as well by those who would repress as by those who would liberate. Jaron Lanier's *Ten Arguments for Deleting Your Social Media Accounts Right Now* (Henry Holt, 2018) takes a more personal view, his principal concerns revolving around the dulling, coarsening, and deadening of the spirit, and the commercial commoditization of the individual, that all too often go along with online living. P. W. Singer and Emerson Booking, in their path-blazing *LikeWar* (Houghton Mifflin Harcourt, 2018), examine thoroughly the ways in which social media can serve a range of forms of conflict. Their expertise in the latest technological advances – from the capacity to create "deep fake" videos to hyper-paced learning capabilities of "chatbots" trained via neural networking – is pretty jaw-dropping.

Last, Andrew Futter, in his *Hacking the Bomb: Cyber Threats and Nuclear Weapons* (Georgetown University Press, 2018) offers nightmarish insights into the vulnerability of the command and control systems that keep the world's atomic-armed powers from "pushing the button" inadvertently. His insights should inform and guide future nuclear arms treaties, fail-safe protocols, and hotlines between national leaders.

Index